THE
HAUNTED
HARLEQUIN

Ghostly Experiences Behind the Scenes

Nikki Folsom

CR

Conflicted Reality Press

Cover Design:	Nikki Folsom & Shawn Kjos
Cover Photography:	Nikki Folsom
Interior Photos:	Interior credits

ISBN-13:	978-0692854280
ISBN-10:	0692854282

Conflicted Reality Press

San Antonio, Texas

Happy Haunting!
Nikki

For our angels who walk with us and those who

watch over us ... .

CONTENTS

NIKKI FOLSOM

INTRODUCTION

Through the years, I have spent of countess hours at the Harlequin fulfilling almost every role available from onstage performer to stage manager to sound technician to light operator to usher. You name it, I have probably volunteered for it. I've been in every room at all times of day losing count of the number of experiences that I've witnessed.

The recollections in this book are those that had the biggest impression on me. I say impression on me specifically because I've experienced exactly the same thing or something similar. Every account shared in this book was either experienced by me, by the person I interviewed, or someone that was present during the event. Incredibly, all recounts except those in the final chapter occurred within the walls of the Harlequin.

Past and present day accounts have been shared in every room of this two-story, historic building. These stories are what formed the structure of this book. Because most experiences were associated with a particular room in the building and almost every room has stories associated with it, I've designed the book as a tour of the building sharing various accounts by room. While some areas are more active than others, you will find stories about each of them sprinkled throughout the book. What makes it odd is that some locations have offered little to no activity to one person, yet an enormous amount of activity to another.

Strangely or not, it seems as though the Harlequin spirits are drawn to certain personalities that enter the building. I'd like to tell you that all the Harlequin spirits are fun loving, theatrical energies who enjoy the company of a fellow thespians; however, that statement would be a lie.

While I have found most of the ghosts are protective and loving energies, there are at least two that are absolutely terrifying. Join me as I introduce you to this amazing theater and the spirits that remain.

CHAPTER

I

My Paranormal Initiation

As you begin reading the experiences compiled in this book, please know that I'm possibly the most curious person you'll ever meet. I ask questions, challenge answers, and insist on looking for the logical explanation in all cases. Being either too nosey or too dumb to know better, I'm typically the first person to walk into a dark room to investigate strange noises or to chase shadow figures. I would most assuredly be the first to die in a slasher movie.

While I am extremely inquisitive, I find that I am also skeptically intuitive. No, no. I'm not Chip Coffee or Amy Allen. They are incredibly gifted psychic mediums that have dedicated their lives to helping people through education, message deliveries, and countless other acts.

For me, the best way to explain "skeptically intuitive" is to say that feelings are impressed upon me regularly, but I second guess myself constantly. All I can tell you is that I know what I feel when I feel it. Simply put, I can sense if energy is giving a good or bad vibration. To be fair, I believe that we all have this ability just some of us choose to embrace it while others suppress it. The gift of freewill allows us this privilege of selection.

Honestly, I understand why some people suppress it. Intuitiveness can be a blessing and a curse. For me, it forces a face to face reality that some things cannot be explained logically. At the same time, it allows me to identify the root causes of "bumps in the night".

I'm not a professional nor would I ever claim to be. That said, I am a witness, therefore a believer. That counts for something. Based on conversations with others throughout the years, I've determined that people generally fall into one of five categories on the "belief" scale, and it swings from extreme to moderate on both ends of the spectrum.

1) **_Extreme Skeptic_** - This is a person who absolutely refuses to believe in the paranormal. Under no circumstance will they even consider the possibility of it. They believe that anyone who takes this seriously is completely naive. The exact way it was put to me was "you're an idiot if you believe in that stuff." Know

anyone in this category?

2) ***Cautious Skeptic*** - This individual is open to the possibility of the paranormal yet dismisses evidence. These are folks who have had genuine paranormal experiences, but are still in denial about it. This is my husband. Imagine the conversations we have in our house.

3) ***Cautious Believers*** - A person who is open to the possibility of the paranormal and actively looks for evidence to support their belief. This is where many of the paranormal experts, researchers, investigators, psychics, mediums, and most "believers" fall. These people have had experiences and they may or may not have evidence to support it. My kids and I fall into this category.

4) ***Extreme Believers*** - A person who is overly eager to believe in the paranormal. These are people who believe everything that happens is a paranormal event even when a logical explanation is provided. While entertaining, they are detrimental to the paranormal field. Who would do that? You'd be surprised. Picture this, a group of pre-teens walk into a supposedly haunted location. All of the sudden, every child within fifty feet is hearing chains rattling and voices groaning.

Yes, there are adults that fall in this category too. You probably know a few.

5) **DKDCers** - Simply put, these individuals approach the paranormal with a "don't know, don't care" attitude. They have either never considered the possibility or are just here to drink with an incredibly fun group of people. I fully appreciate these types of people because, at least, I know they're honest. Personally, I spent the first five years of my life as a DKDCer. I was too young to consider the paranormal a possibility.

At five years old, I was what some would call a "tomboy." The only thing that interested me was working in the garden with my grandfather and out-running the boys in the neighborhood. The best way to describe me at that time was happy, outgoing, curious, and fearless. Maybe I was all of those things because I don't recall seeing or hearing anything I could not explain.

My parents and I lived in south central Pennsylvania in a one story ranch home with a large basement. Three of the rooms were "fixed off" meaning they had carpet and were used regularly. This home was special to all of us because my Dad and Papa helped build it. It was in this house at five years of age that I moved from the "DKDC" category to a "Cautious Believer".

It was in the middle of a fall night. Snow was not yet covering the ground, but it was too cold outside for the windows to be open.

Sleeping soundly in my bedroom, I woke suddenly to the sound of a strange swooshing noise in the hallway. My eyes shot open so fast that they burned. I remember blinking numerous times to ease the pain. After my eyes adjusted, I tried to refocused on the noise.

At the time, my bedroom door was fully open exposing the dark hallway. My small nightlight illuminated a large part of my room near the hall giving just enough light for me to reassure myself that everything was okay. Hearing and seeing nothing, I laid back and attempted to go back to sleep.

Suddenly, I heard it again.

I sat straight up in bed and looked into the hallway expecting one of my parents to walk in.

After what seemed like an eternity of gazing at the doorway, someone walked past it. It was a soldier. He wore a strange uniform with his light trousers tucked into his dark boots. His upper body had a dark long-sleeved jacket with light fabric criss-crossed over his chest. In his hand, he carried an odd-looking rifle with a knife on the end. At five years old, I had no idea what a bayonet was nor did I know how they were used.

I didn't scream at first. I just stared at the doorway confused. Did I really see a soldier? Why was there a soldier in my house? Why was he dressed so funny?

Thinking my eyes were playing tricks on me, I rubbed them then looked back at the door. Even then, my young mind was trying to apply logic to the situation. It wasn't until the soldier walked back past the door that I realized what I saw was real. I screamed like my ass was on fire and as loud as my vocal cords would allow. Within seconds, my mom came running to my room. She did her best to calm me down but could not explain what I had seen.

That, my friends, is where my journey into the paranormal began. To this day, I sleep with a nightlight. Funny tidbit as I look back now, a soldier apparition would be quite appropriate as our old house was roughly twenty miles from the battlefield in Gettysburg, Pennsylvania.

Since that soldier's visit many years ago, I've experienced an array of unexplainable activities all over the world.

One of the most active places for me is The Harlequin, previously known as the Harlequin Dinner Theater, on Fort Sam Houston in San Antonio, Texas. I realize that a person can go to any city in any country and find a theater with a "ghost story." For me, this place is different because I have seen, heard, and felt things with my own senses here.

I was introduced to the Harlequin in the summer of 2009. My youngest daughter, Ashton, had been invited to a children's theater summer camp by her best friend since second grade, Samantha Eberle. Samantha is a beautiful young lady and like another daughter to me. (As a side note, Ash and Sam are still best friends after all these years.)

Because I've always loved the theater and knowing the support this kind of a community offers, I was thrilled to see Ashton take an interest. We gathered everything she could possibly need for the first day and made our way to the theater. I had barely stepped through the front doors when I felt "it." While I can't explain specifically what "it" was, I can describe the feeling that surrounded me - thick, musty air. It wasn't threatening but not peaceful either. I guess the best way to describe my feeling was cautious but curious.

Being the first day of camp, kids and parents were everywhere. Ashton and I walked into the lobby and greeted the organizers. I signed some papers, met some of the other kids, then kissed Ashton goodbye. She quickly scurried off with her new friends. I'm not sure why, but I felt a sense of comfort knowing that she would have a great time building relationships, exploring her talent, and learning about theater.

As I walked out of the theater toward the car, I remember turning back momentarily. I'm not sure if I was subconsciously warning the energies to leave her alone or asking the spirits to protect her. Maybe, I was a just nervous mother leaving her baby girl.

As I began to spend more time at the Harlequin, I realized that my initial feeling of caution was spot on. There is definitely more in the building than what the eye can see. Every room has a presence within it and spirits with varying personalities roam the halls.

CHAPTER

2

Welcome to the Harlequin

Walking up to the front door of a theater evokes a sense of excitement. For performers, it's the adrenaline filled energy they feel before stepping onto the stage and pouring their heart into the performance. For patrons, it's a glimmer of hope anticipating a song or a line that will resurrect a forgotten memory or spark the flame of a dream abandoned long ago.

Speaking from experience, live theater is no place for the weak. The audience is forced to focus, feel, and appreciate art coming to life before their very eyes. In most cases, it offers a two hour escape from reality and emersion into a make-believe world of someone else's life. Eyes are fixated on the stage, enjoying each moment and preparing for the next scene in the story.

At the Harlequin, live theater takes on a completely different meaning. When the stage is lit and the action is unfolding, spirits move among the living as they reminisce of their days in the spotlight. When the curtain is closed and the chairs are empty, unfathomable and sometimes frightening stories are unfolding behind the scenes.

Located in San Antonio on Fort Sam Houston, The Harlequin is one of 900 buildings spread across 400 acres. Fort Sam, one of the oldest Army installations in the United States, was established in 1870.

Up until 1845, Republic of Texas troops fought against Indian warriors and Mexican soldiers over the ownership of the land. For many turbulent years, battles blazed between the three groups. Finally in 1845, the Republic of Texas was drained financially and decided the best course of action was to become part of the United States.

When US troops arrived in Texas in 1846, they didn't have an official "base" until the city of San Antonio donated 92 acres to the United States Army in 1870.

In 1876, the very first building on Fort Sam was built - The Quadrangle. After three years of construction, it was completed in 1879. The Quadrangle still stands as proud and as powerful as it the day it was opened one hundred and thirty eight years ago. Interestingly enough, this area has it's own ghost stories to tell, but that is for another time.

All Texans know the story of the Alamo and the battle for independence between Mexico and the Republic of Texas. Along with these brave men, many Native Americans also fought and lost land in these battles. Win or lose, each warrior gave everything they had to fight for the land they desperately desired. Much respect is felt for every person the world lost in these battles. The historic Alamo is located 4.6 miles from Fort Sam.

As I researched the history of Fort Sam Houston, I discovered an interesting fact that confirms the Native American presence on the land and their never-ending fight for existence.

In 1886, Geronimo and his constituents were held at the Quadrangle for approximately thirty days before US troops were charged with transferring him to a military base in Florida. Geronimo's presence along with archeological finds on the base validates several of the sightings across the fort and at the Harlequin.

Erected in 1943, the Harlequin building was built as a Non-Commissioned Officers (NCO) Club offering three bars, two upstairs and one downstairs; a swimming pool, now filled in; a dance hall; meeting spots for social clubs; and plenty of space for special events. This particular NCO Club closed when a new and improved NCO Club was build a few blocks away; however, the vacant World War II era building wasn't empty for long.

Fort Sam Houston NCO Club in 1967
Photo Credit: United States Army

The Army developed a brilliant music program offering lessons, instrument rental, and individual space for soldiers to learn or expand their knowledge of their choice in musical instruments. These activities continued until 1974.

In April of 1975, the building was repurposed, opening as the Harlequin Dinner Theater. Its first production was *Goodbye Charlie*.

For almost thirty-five years, this theater was managed by the dynamic duo of Bruce Shirky and Florence Bunton. Bruce led the artistic direction while Florence managed the operations. The business ran like a well-oiled machine, offering approximately eight live productions a year. All flowed smoothly until 1979.

Because San Antonio is in the far south, we don't have cold weather as often or as severe as our northern friends. This means that when a cold front hits, it hits hard; sometimes when we least expect it.

On the night of January 2, 1979, a major cold front was making its way through south Texas. Unfortunately, Fort Sam Houston was directly in the cross-hairs. With many structures built thirty or more years ago, every building on base was at risk.

At the Harlequin, the pipes couldn't handle the incredibly low temperatures and began to freeze triggering the sprinkler system to kick on. Water fell from the sprinklers throughout the building for eight hours before it was discovered. By the time Florence arrived the next morning, the entire building was flooded. Little did she know, luck was on her side.

Across the base, numerous buildings were dealt worse cards. Pipes burst in several buildings flooding out the insides and creating unstable structures. Orders were given for these buildings to be demolished. Luckily for the Harlequin, the Army chose to restore it.

The theater went through a clean-up and remodel project from 1979 though 1982. During those three years, Bruce and Florence never stopped producing plays. They coordinated and performed in other spaces on base and even featured some touring shows.

When Bruce and Florence made the decision to retire in 2009, they worried that all the joy the Harlequin had offered so many people would be lost. While there were a few bumps in the road, their dream was not lost and the Harlequin Dinner Theater continued producing live shows, maintaining a consistent performance streak for forty-two straight years which is still going strong today.

Now known as The Harlequin, the theater no longer offers dinner, but the shows are as magnificent as ever. Overseen by two of the most incredible people I've ever met - Robert Olivas and Shawn Kjos, this theater amazes me every time I walk through the doors.

Robert is the Facilities Manager and responsible for coordinating, directing and sometimes performing in of all the plays. Shawn is the Operations Manager who flawlessly creates, directs and performs in the Harlequin's original musical revues. This wonderful place is a beloved theater in the San Antonio community.

Sadly, we lost Bruce in 2015, but his commitment to this theater and his memory will live on forever. Our precious Florence still stops by every once in while to say hi to everyone at the Harlequin. Whether a person is alive or in spirit, her greeting is genuine; her energy warms every heart, and her smile lights up the room.

For many years, multiple accounts have been passed down of disembodied voices, soft touches, unexplainable noises, strange footsteps, creepy shadow figures, full bodied apparitions, and the list goes on and on.

In 2011, a local San Antonio news show ran a story on the hauntings at Fort Sam Houston. Brad and Barry Klinge, stars of "Ghost Lab" and founders of the San Antonio based "Everyday Paranormal," even joined the news crew in their visit. The newscaster could not have been any nicer or more professional to the employees and volunteers when they spent time with us.

Happy to share some experiences and give accounts of rumored history, I took the news crew on a tour of the facility. Brad and Barry were able to give additional background based on their research and experiences, too. For me, I was thrilled just to be able to give the spirits a voice.

After the visit, the newscaster conducted her own investigation into the background of the theater. Despite her research with the historical society, she was unable to uncover any documentation to validate our rumored histories. With no supporting data, she discounted the numerous experiences we shared with her. Her final report gave the impression that the things we experienced had not really happened. Sound familiar?

I would categorize her as a "cautious skeptic." In fairness, it's her job to disregard anything that isn't black and white. Wouldn't it be nice if the world really worked like that?

Along with other locations that experience unexplainable activity, there are back stories that give a jaded reason for these tales. Some of these stories have been received from people who were there or from mediums who walked through the building.

I would like to say that I have documented proof confirming the validity every one of these accounts; however, I've discovered that most records of these back stories don't exist. Believe me when I say military bases are not the easiest places to uncover documented accounts of not-so-pleasant activities.

What I can tell you is that the Harlequin has quite the reputation on base. Military Police, maintenance men, emergency vehicles, and any other person coming to patrol or service equipment will not come to the building alone. They always arrive in pairs.

While I typically would not share rumored back stories without documentation, I need to do so in this case. As I stated earlier, this is a military base. Who knows how things are documented? Maybe I wasn't looking in the right place. Maybe I was looking for a murder when I should have been looking for an accident or a suicide. Maybe activities were covered up to protect careers, marriages, futures, etc.

Either way, I want you to be aware of the stories that have been passed down. One day, I would love to invite other mediums to walk through the building to give us their impressions directly. It would certainly be an interesting approach to send them in with no background. Hopefully, they could validate the stories for us or tell us the truth of the situation.

The Back Stories

Based on documented experiences and witness interviews, there are many spirits roaming the building. Some stay in a general area while others have been seen in multiple places. Maybe they are always moving around and we don't realize it. That said, please know that I don't believe that these spirits are the only entities wandering about the theater.

The first spirit is a child - a little girl. Through investigations and experience, we believe her youthful energy puts her age at somewhere between six and nine. She seems to be a lovely young lady with no ill intent whatsoever. Her laughter is heartwarming and her presence gives a sense of childlike excitement.

The rumored story associated with her is quite sad. It's said that she was swimming in the NCO swimming pool one afternoon and tragically drowned. Some have even go so far as to say that her death was the reason the pool was filled in.

Along with the little girl, there was once a little boy roaming the halls. Less is known about him. When Florence worked at the Harlequin, she invited two of her psychic medium friends to walk through the building. Christine, one of the friends, indicated that she could see the boy with knee-high pants and a newsboy hat. She received the impression that he died of scarlet fever.

The lad hasn't been seen in quite some time. Florence told me that several years ago one of the mediums in the building conducted a ritual to cross over any spirit that wished to go into the light. Maybe the little boy took that opportunity to move on? We may never know.

During the same walk with Florence, Christine indicated that a Native American man was present. He seemed to prefer hanging around the bottom of the stairs. Christine explained that he was a scout for the Army and brought to Fort Sam. After arriving, he was used, abused then thrown into jail. He died of neglect - no food or water.

Brad and Barry Klinge snagged a photograph of the another spirit seen at the Harlequin. Known affectionately as the "bartender," this tall, dark haired gentleman wears a white shirt and black pants.

While I can't say that he is an actual bartender, the only place he is ever seen is around the bar area hence the name bartender. Most sightings of him are so brief that any energy he exudes is unfelt. Typically, witnesses are left more confused than anything.

The "green lady" spirit has only been seen once upstairs at the Harlequin; however, it's possible that she is the female voice heard around the theater quite frequently.

The green lady, whose name is Minnie, was once an usher for the theater. At 4 feet 10 inches, Minnie was small yet mighty.

Florence described her as a firecracker of a lady who wouldn't take any crap from anyone.

Portrait of the "green lady", Minnie.
Photo by: Nikki Folsom

Because of her time investment at the theater, a portrait was painted of her and it still hangs in the Rehearsal Room upstairs.

Another interesting spirit roaming the theater is a gentleman we call "the gray haired man." Generally seen in the kitchen and dining room area, he doesn't give any impression that he is around. Those of us that see him get a glimpse of him out of the corner of our eye. He doesn't approach anyone and simply watches the living from afar.

We don't know for sure who our gray-haired man is, but we have a few leads. Rummaging through the light booth one day, Robert found an old picture of a performer from many years ago. He certainly matches the sightings. Another contender for the title was a director at the Harlequin in the seventies. A patron dropped off an old program one day. In it, we found a picture of a man that definitely looks like the gray-haired specter as well.

Either of these individuals could be a twin to the "gray haired man." I'm not saying they are one and the same; however, I would say there is a possibility.

Our "invisible" woman spirit has never been seen. At least, we don't think so although she has been felt on numerous occasions.

The hand-me-down history is from the NCO Club era. Apparently, a waitress was having an affair with one of the married officers. No one was ever found to be responsible for her death. All that was said is that she was found murdered in the music room upstairs.

Typically, she has a very protective energy. People who have encountered her feel a sense of security because every time she comes around she's attempting to warn them about something. Women specifically tend to feel an energy surround them like a bubble of protection especially if a threatening presence is close by. This threatening presence is our next spirit, the "mean man."

His backstory as told by one of the mediums is quite simple. He was a soldier who was killed in a shoot-out while drinking at the upstairs NCO bar. While he is upstairs most of the time, I personally believe that he has ventured downstairs on occasion because his energy is almost recognizable at this point. The air around you becomes terribly thick, leaving you dripping with a heavy sense of intimidation.

Many years ago, Dorin Finn visited the theater. Dorin is a friend of mine and also happens to be a sensitive. During her visit, she was walking down the stairs and was pushed. She felt that it was a masculine entity with a threatening personality. Certainly sounds like the energy of the man we have all come to recognize.

One of the most frightening entities at that theater is what we call "the creature." There are no other words for it because we don't have a name that would properly categorize this unknown being. It's terrifying and has been sighted in at least three areas of the building - the light booth, backstage, and the grid. It gives you the feeling that you are being watched by a predator as it stalks its prey.

Unfortunately, I don't have a backstory on this entity. God only knows where it came from and why it's here. Its appearance looks to be more like an elemental or even alien than of an apparition. All I can tell you is that I don't wish this presence on anyone.

In addition to the entities referenced previously, the theater has more than one shadow person. I've lost count of the sightings and experiences with them. While I'll capture some encounters with them in this book, I assure you there are a hundred more where these came from. These shadow figures are aggressive and unnerving. They make certain they are seen by the person they are watching.

Standing anywhere from six to seven feet tall, they are solid black figures in the shape of a human with zero detailed features - faceless, eyeless entities whose vacant stare burns through the flesh humans leaving them terrified and helpless. As for a back story, I have nothing. Are they shadow versions of the entities that exist at the Harlequin? What is their intention? I have no idea.

Another interesting piece to the puzzle is that some of the

spirits are seen or heard regularly while others are seen infrequently. We have not been able to identify any correlation to sightings or frequencies.

While it is easy to dismiss the Harlequin stories as old wives tales, it is not so simple when you witnesses the activity right before your eyes. Every eyewitness account documented in this book is 100% true. I appreciate that some may not be able to grasp another individual's paranormal experience. That is acceptable even understandable; however, discounting a person's experience because you didn't see it yourself is close-minded and sad.

CHAPTER

3

Downstairs

Approaching the Harlequin, patrons and performers enter through the double-doored entry at the front of the building. The first floor of the theater is comprised of seven main areas - lobby, box office, bar and lounge area, kitchen, house, backstage, and the stage.

Upon entering, you are standing in the theater's main lobby, a small carpeted area for mingling before the house a.k.a. dining room opens. To your left, there's a small box office window usually manned by one of a handful of people.

Beside the box office is a set of curtains leading to the upstairs, and directly in front of you is another set of curtains that welcomes patrons to the house. To the left of the house entryway, you find an entrance to the kitchen area and to the right, you will see the double-door entry into the bar and lounge area.

During the day, one or two people are working at the theater. The number of people working depends on the day of the week and the number of activities that need to get done pre-show. When two people are there, one will be working in the box office responding to reservation requests, answering customer phone calls, and readying tickets for the show. Meanwhile, the other individual is setting up the tables in the house, fixing costumes, adjusting lights, editing music, and/or caring for general building management.

The positive side of having two people in the building is that any unexplained activity can be discussed, validated, even investigated immediately. While the experience could be uncomfortable, we aren't alone and can get immediate confirmation of our sanity. It's the days when we are alone at the theater that can be most unsettling.

Heard Our Names

One afternoon, Robert arrived for his solo shift at the theater. He made his way into the box office, created his list of action items for the day, and sat down at the computer to check his email.

After focusing for about thirty minutes, he was distracted by the sound of a name being called. He looked around. Remembering that he was alone in the building and that it was the middle of the day, he assumed that a group of soldiers were outside talking.

Knowing there were quite a few critical tasks to be completed, he refocused on his email.

Within a few minutes, he heard the voice again. This time, he could have sworn it was a man calling his name. Thinking that he needed a break, he went to the wait station, made himself some coffee, then walked to the front door to take a quick look outside. It was a beautiful day. He noticed a few people across the base moving around, but no one was near the theater.

With a fresh cup of coffee, he sat back down to begin working on the reservation list. Suddenly, he was startled by a loud and firm yell "ROBERT!" that seemed to be coming from the lobby. He shot up from his chair and raced into the lobby sure someone would be standing there. No one. Concerned someone was in the building that he didn't know about, he proceeded into the lounge, then walked the entire perimeter of the building inside and out. No one was anywhere to be found.

Robert is a "cautious believer." He will go to every length to investigate the source of unexplained events; however, he's had enough experiences to know that sometimes there is no explanation. This was one of those times.

On another day, Shawn was scheduled to work alone during the afternoon. Driving to work, he was organizing his thoughts so he would have a mental checklist upon arrival. He decided that he would prepare the house area first then take care of the activities in the box office. Arriving at approximately noon, he unlocked the front doors and walked into the box office. He barely sat his computer bag down when he heard Robert's voice call out his name.

"Shawn!"

"What?" Shawn responded.

Silence.

That's when it hit him. Robert wasn't there. Slightly unnerved and grasping to confirm his sanity, he called Robert's cell phone.

"Hello," Robert said.

"Where are you?" Shawn asked.

"Home. Making myself a sandwich. Why?" Robert responded.

Confused, yet not wanting to alarm Robert, Shawn calmly ended the conversation with him and turned on music to drown out any additional voices that might come through.

Knowing these odd occurrences can rattle anyone's comfort level, I asked both Shawn and Robert how they are able to keep working when things like that happen.

"Work still needs to get done," Robert explained.

"Because there is no immediate threat, the only action you can take in situations like these is to ignore it," Shawn added.

"I don't know what I'd do if it were me in that situation," I told them.

Fast forward a month or two, I was sitting at the soundboard in the houses while the cast was working on choreography on stage. The music was turned off, so the cast could hear Sarah Peters, our beautiful soprano and choreographer, teaching the dance steps.

When the cast is focusing on dancing, I could be doing one of a thousand things - fixing costumes, tinkering with microphones, researching something online, organizing somewhere in the theater, even scrolling through Facebook.

That night, I was focused on the soundboard settings and Shawn was watching the cast on stage from about the middle of the house. Suddenly, I heard "Nikki" come from the lounge. My head shot up looking around to see who yelled my name. Shawn noticed me jerk my head up quickly.

"What?" he said.

"Did you just call my name?" I asked.

"No," he said.

That's when it dawned on me. Everyone was on the stage except Shawn who was in front of me and the voice came from behind me in the lounge. Confused, I looked at Shawn then to the lounge door then back to Shawn. He could read my facial expression like a seer can read tea leaves.

Before I said a word, he and I were both headed to the lounge. As expected, there was no one there. Now, I understand what it feels like to hear a disembodied voice call out your name.

Hearing your name being called is a fairly common

occurrence for several of us. Maybe the spirits get to know your name then call out for you. Who knows? I can tell you that there are at least three of us that this happens to on a regular basis. It is equally unnerving every time it occurs.

The creepiest part about this particular experience is that it has evolved. Robert has heard his name called out by his own voice. The entity somehow mimics the voice of the person they are calling out to. I would love to capture this on a recorder somehow. Unfortunately, these types of occurrences happen randomly making it nearly impossible.

Shadows in the Lobby

One of most common things you can see around the theater is shadows. They vary in shape, size, color, even texture. On a fairly regular basis though, they can be seen moving through the lobby area. I can't count the number of times we say to each other, "Did you see that?" Several times, the shadows have appeared when a person in the lounge or dining room happened to be looking into the lobby area.

The Harlequin lobby from the front doors of the building.
Photo Credit: Nikki Folsom

One time, a large white mass approximately seven feet high was seen moving from up center stage to up stage right. Fifteen minutes later, that same white mass was moving through the lobby and toward the box office stairs. This entity could be considered a shadow figure because it slightly resembles a human form.

Another common sighting is a small black mass that appears separately but follows the same path as the large white figure. Standing at about three to four feet high, this mass looks like a ball of black smoke moving around the room and darting around corners. A strange yet possibly relevant coincidence is that I have seen this same small black mass at my house. (See Dark Mass at my House in Chapter 18)

Every occurrence reported about these shadows at the theater indicates that the visual on them has lasted for less than five seconds and neither entity acknowledges the presence of people. They just move about as if they have somewhere to be. The mass at my house was different. It didn't have eyes, but I know it knew I was there. I felt the intimidation factor coming from it. In any case, a skeptic would say that it is simply an issue with a human eye. I would accept this explanation if it wouldn't happen so often to so many people.

The Tall Shadow

A shadow experience that I cannot explain happened to me in March 2016. During rehearsals for the upcoming production of *The Gingerbread Lady,* the cast was on stage running through a scene. I had some time before I was needed on stage and decided to run my lines to myself in the lounge. With two continuously open doors, it makes it very easy to view anyone passing through the lobby.

Because I'm me, I cannot sit still. Ever. With that, I walked around the lounge as I recited my lines out loud. Moving through the tables, I heard a slight movement in the lobby and looked up. I remember stopping my line mid-sentence with my mouth still hanging open.

Directly across from me in the lobby, an extremely tall shadow moving abruptly from the direction of the house entryway across the lobby towards the box office curtains. The transparent shadow was white with no discernible features. It stood about seven feet tall and was in my view for less than three seconds.

Before I could react, it disappeared. I didn't feel threatened at all, but I got a sense that I should not attempt to follow it. After multiple experiences in my life of ignoring my gut and paying the price for it, I've learned to listen to my instincts especially in situations like this.

I walked into the theater and quietly told Robert about what I had just witnessed. That's when I discovered that he had seen the same figure walk across the stage about fifteen minutes before I saw it.

CHAPTER

4

Lounge

Right off the lobby is one of the favorite places in the theater - the lounge. It offers a fun, friendly atmosphere with good people and great drinks. The room consists of twenty-four tables that seat between four to six people, a fully stocked bar, a set of restrooms, a storage room, and a piano area. Even as an NCO Club, this lounge was used as a bar area.

During the Vietnam era, the building served as a music center. The lounge was set up with soundproof modules allowing the soldiers to come to the building, check out a musical instrument, and go to one of the modules to play their chosen instrument.

When the Harlequin Dinner Theater opened in the seventies, the sound modules remained in this area. Most of the time, the room went unused except for the occasional storage needs that popped up.

Closed off from most traffic in and out of the theater, the area sat quiet. It wasn't until the remodel of 1982 that the room was converted back to its original purpose - a lounge. The refreshed area came with an added bonus of new restrooms. These new features revitalized the room making it the "go to" area to hang out before and after shows.

On show nights before the house opens, you'll find a fun crowd of people sharing stories while music plays softly in the background. During dark days (non show nights), this area is used for rehearsals, cast parties, birthday parties, costume walks, show development, auditions, cabaret, and any other miscellaneous meeting you can think of. Because the Harlequin is supported by a close knit theater family, we frequently spend time together in the lounge.

The lounge during a recent rehearsal.
Photo credit: Nikki Folsom

Interestingly enough, most experiences in this room occur when someone is alone. Notice that I said "most" experiences - not all. As an example, the lounge sits directly below the long hallway and several rooms upstairs. Many times when we are sitting in the lounge running music, conducting read-thrus or just socializing, we can hear footsteps running overhead. We are all fully aware that no one is upstairs yet we clearly hear what sounds like children playfully skipping around.

The Bartender

The lounge is the location where bartender is regularly seen. Quite honestly, he has been seen more often than I realized when I started the book. This nondescript looking gentleman was photographed by Brad and Barry Klinge when they investigated the theater several years ago. Their picture shows a man sitting in a chair on the left side of the lounge.

While the Klinge brothers saw him in the photograph, several of the regular cast members have seen him in person. One of those cast members is Matt Tejeda.

Matt is a fun loving guy known for making people laugh, playing his guitar, and enjoying a good practical joke - like the time when we were in the middle of an incredibly powerful dramatic scene. Matt decided to insert some improvised comedy causing the entire cast to break into laughter onstage. He keeps us all on our toes and we love him dearly for it.

During rehearsals for *A Few Good Men* in May 2012, Matt was coming into the dining room for rehearsal.

"Who is the dude with the top hat at the bar?" he said.

Knowing his sense of humor, I assumed he was messing with me and called him out on his question.

"Shut up. Stop lying," I said.

Matt looked at me confused as to why I would assume he wasn't telling the truth. I told him that he was just saying that because of the ghost story. He had no idea what I was talking about. Before I could say another word, he ran back in the lounge.

When he returned to the dining room a few seconds later, all he could say was, "He's gone." I'll never forget the look of confusion on his face. Apparently, he had looked all over the lounge and found nothing. Of course, he heard stories about the ghosts at the Harlequin, but had never before heard about the bartender.

Unexplained Burn

In June 2016, the Harlequin was showing an original summer musical, *Those Oldies but Goodies*, which was filled with all the fifties music you could handle. The spirits of the Harlequin seem to love this era. Every time we do a fifties show, the activity tends to pick up and the spirits seem happier with the exception of the "mean man." Most of the time, he tends to stay upstairs.

One Friday night after the show, Shawn was closing down the bar, cleaning the counter, and talking to Suzy Bianchi-Barrett, co-mom to our incredible, Sarah. All of the sudden, his neck felt like it was on fire. Behind the bar is a large mirror, so Shawn moved closer to it to get a better look at what could be causing his pain. There, on his neck, was a huge red mark.

Robert came in from the box office to take a look at it, then talked with Shawn and Suzy to try to come up with what could have cause the sudden redness. Shawn explained that he was cleaning with water so there was nothing that could have irritated his neck. After exploring all possibilities and finding no explanation for the pain, everyone decided it was a fluke and went home.

The next morning, Shawn woke up with his neck still burning. When he looked in the mirror, he discovered a burn mark approximately one inch long. He was so taken back by the burn that he took a snapshot and sent it to me. Thank God he did because now we have documentation of it. I've seen

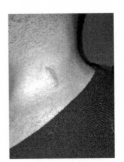

The burns from nowhere.
Photo Credit: Shawn Kjos

burns like that years ago when I burned my neck with a curling iron; however, it isn't normal for something like that to come out of thin air.

The White Mist

Performing on stage at the Harlequin is a family affair for the Folsoms. My daughter, Ashton sticks to the musicals because she has a strong, beautiful voice. My husband, Eric manages the spotlight and I focus on the plays because I know my strengths. I've seen the singers in the Harlequin musicals. They are pretty damn incredible, so for musicals, I stay at the soundboard where I belong. On occasion, I enjoy performing in some of the plays.

Many times during play rehearsals, Ashton will come along with me to the theater. Knowing her sensitivity, you'd think that she would avoid the theater when she doesn't have to be there. Nope, it's the complete opposite for her. She loves being there. It's her sanctuary. The Harlequin has always been her escape from the craziness of school bullies, teenage drama, and life's crap in general. Most of the time when she goes with me, she spends the time in the lounge and focuses on her homework.

During rehearsal for *The Gingerbread Lady* in 2016, Ashton was in the lounge alone while Robert, Priscilla, Ashley and I rehearsed for the opening of our show. Seated at the table closest to the lobby, Ashton was working on her school work while her latest tunes blared through her headphones.

After some time, she started to get that nagging feeling in her stomach that something was nearby. Within a few seconds, she sensed the energy was directly in front of her. Because she didn't feel threatened, she decided to try to ignore it hoping it would go away. She successfully fought it off for about thirty seconds.

Finally, the urge to look up overpowered her and she raised her head slowly. There floating in front of her was a large, white, cloud-like mist. No face, no details just a semi-transparent mist. She was mesmerized by it for about ten seconds, then it just disappeared right before her eyes. Feeling no sense of dread or fear, she put her head back down and went back to her homework.

Disembodied Breathing

On many occasions throughout the theater, countless incidents of breathing have been reported by patrons, volunteers, performers, and employees. They range from sighs to gasps of breath being felt on one's ear. Unfortunately, there is not much you can do with the reports except document them.

On rare occasions, you are able to discern a gender but for the most part, breath is as gender neutral and non-specific as it comes. One breathing incident was reported from 2010 in the lounge.

It was late spring of 2010 and rehearsal had just begun for the summer show. The cast was gathered around a table directly in the lounge from the lobby. They had been singing for quite some time. Realizing they needed some vocal rest, the director gave them a ten minute break. No one moved, but they all went silent for a moment. Shawn was sitting with his right ear facing the lobby while another male cast member sat directly across from him.

As he looked down to see what the next song was, Shawn heard a loud, heavy sigh in his right ear. He looked up immediately. Before he could speak, the cast member directly across from him was reacting because he heard the exact same sigh in his left ear. It was like a spirit leaned in-between them and exhaled loudly.

Knock, Knock

A few years ago, we had a wonderful lady named Gerry who tended the bar during shows. After every show, she would close out the bar register while Robert closed out the box office. One night after a show, Robert happened to be helping Gerry as she closed out for the night. They were both situated behind the bar with Gerry washing glasses while Robert balanced the bar register.

Suddenly, there was a loud, heavy pounding on the emergency exit door across the room. Thinking it was a lost soldier or someone playing a trick, Robert quickly ran to the door and flung it open. No one was there. He walked out, looked around then came back in to finish his work for the night.

Shrugging their shoulders and assuming it was nothing, they went back to counting the money and finishing the close procedures. All of the sudden an eerie silence came across the bar followed by a heavy and overwhelming sense of dread. They looked at each other then looked around the room. Within seconds, they felt surrounded, threatened and overwhelmed.

Robert is another one of the highly sensitive people at the Harlequin and he knows to listen to the guidance given. He immediately sensed that someone or something was out to do them harm. Knowing they were in danger and wanting to protect Gerry, Robert took action.

"We're leaving," he said.

Robert secured the building from the inside. They both quickly grabbed their stuff and exited as fast as they could.

As they reached the door, Robert turned back and told the energies that they are not welcome to follow and must remain in the building. As soon as they stepped outside, the threatening sensation was gone, leaving them both enormously relieved.

On many nights, I find myself leaving the theater the same time Robert and Shawn do. Every single night, Robert tells the spirits that they must not follow anyone out of the theater. After all the things that we have seen, I think that is an excellent practice.

Shaking Shelves

No matter who you talk to, the Harlequin is known as a creepy building. It seems like every person who ever stepped inside has a story that makes you question your sanity. One such story happened many years ago when Bruce and Florence were overseeing the building.

One night, the Military Police were conducting their normal nightly patrol around the base. Part of their routine involved randomly checking buildings to ensure they were secure.

As they passed the theater, one of the soldiers began to share some of the ghost stories frequently whispered about the Harlequin. Feeling brave with two of them, they decided to pull in, take a walk around the building, and double check the doors. When they reached the side kitchen door, they pressed on the door handle and pulled. To their surprise, the door opened. Immediately, they went into protection mode concerned that someone may have broken into the building.

They entered slowly and made their way down the dark kitchen hallway passing the laundry area, then the dishwashing room. As they reached the lobby, the light of the moon was coming in the front window paneled doors.

Immediately, they saw eyes looking at them. They jumped. Startled yet composed, one of the MPs shined a flashlight in the direction of the eyes. It was the portrait of Minnie. Relieved, they laughed nervously to each other and continued with their check of the building.

Not knowing the inside of the building, they moved into the first set of open doors to the right of the portrait which led them into the lounge area. As soon as they stepped through the entrance, the glass shelves holding the bar glasses began shaking violently.

Terrified, they ran out the building the same way they had entered it and called Bruce. When he arrived, the MPs were waiting in their car refusing to go into the building without him. Bruce did an entire walkthrough of the building with the MPs in tow. They found no one there and nothing missing.

Man in the Mirror

In an early 2009 vocal rehearsal, a cast of six and the director at the time sat around a lounge table rehearsing songs for an upcoming show. Because the theater was closed for the evening and the cast could not be interrupted, the front door was locked.

At this rehearsal, Johnny Halpenny happened to be sitting in the seat facing the mirrored back wall of the lounge. The reflection allowed him to see anything happening in the lobby behind him.

As they sang, Johnny was distracted by movement in the mirror. When he looked toward it, a tall Caucasian man was looking back at him. They locked eyes for a few seconds - enough time for Johnny to gather a great description of him. He was approximately six feet tall with dark hair, sideburns and facial hair. Johnny also noticed that the man was wearing a white shirt with dark pleated pants.

"How old do you think he was?" I asked.

"My best guess is that he was in his forties or fifties," Johnny replied.

After their brief stare down, the man simply turned and walked away. The director noticed the confusion on Johnny's face and stopped the music. Then, the cast noticed.

"What's wrong?" they said.

"I saw the man," Johnny replied as he pointed to the lobby.

"What man?" they said.

Everyone in the cast turned to look, but no one was there. They all got up and proceeded to check the theater for the man. No one was found and the front door remained locked. All Johnny could tell them was that he was standing right in front of the double doorway from the lobby to the lounge. There was no sense of danger only a curious energy then it was gone.

> *The chairs in the lounge are casters meaning they have wheels on them. Johnny shared with me that one night during a rehearsal, one of the chairs across the room began to move on its own. Because the floor is carpeted, chairs don't move unless someone or something moves them. He immediately investigated and found nothing that could explain the movement.*

CHAPTER
5
Kitchen

Because the Harlequin once served meals on a regular basis, it has a full service kitchen with all the bells and whistles of a commercial restaurant. It's comprised of six different areas - the kitchen, laundry area, dishwashing room, wait station, the buffet area, and a restroom.

While the actual kitchen area has quite a bit of activity, it is usually heard and not seen. For example, objects can be heard moving fairly often, yet no one is in the room.

On numerous occasions, the cast will be sitting in the house during rehearsals and hear a noise that sounds like utensils, pots, or plates moving around. At times, it even sounds like a person walking around or even singing back there. After we all listen for a moment, we try to identify a logical explanation. If we come up with none, we investigate. Every single time, we find nothing.

Occasionally, shadows have been seen fluttering around but not something that is identifiable. It simply looks like a dark shadows. As quickly as they appear, they are gone.

The Dapper Gentleman

During the 1979-1982 refurbishment of the Harlequin, Bruce and Florence worked with the Army to improve the presentation and food quality offered by the dinner theater. With that, Fort Sam approved a budget that supported hiring an executive chef and a cook.

After sifting through many candidates, both positions were filled. Bonnie, the new cook, ran the kitchen. She was quick, efficient and did her job well. Every show day, she would get to the theater, put her belongings down, turn on the kitchen lights, and make her way through the kitchen door to the light switch that illuminated the buffet and tech area. Entering the buffet area, she was always a bit cautious because there were times that someone was waiting for her.

Buffet area wall into the tech room.
Photo Credit: Cameron Kofoet

On those occasions, Bonnie would walk through the kitchen

door into the darkened area and see a man casually leaning up against the wall where the tech room started. Looking like he just stepped out of a gangster movie, he wore a suit, a fedora, and had a coat slung over his one shoulder held by the pointer finger on his hand. His visits didn't last long. As soon as he saw her, he would tip his hat, turn around, walk toward backstage, and disappear.

The first time she saw him, Bonnie ran to the light switch, flipped it to the on position, and ran backstage looking for the mystery fellow. Finding nothing, she went back to her work in the kitchen.

Strangely, his visitation did not frighten her. It was just another energy stopping in to say hi. When he made any appearances after the first one, she knew better than to go check. He would not be there.

Dish Room Mist

The dishwashing room is a small, stand-alone area off the kitchen hallway right off the lobby. Months ago when dinner was still being served, the room was much busier than it is today. When in use, only one person was able to fit in the room because of the stacks of dishes, glasses, and silverware piled up for the start of the wash and dry process.

Now, the room is used to wash bar glasses and miscellaneous items. Rarely if ever does anything happen in the room while people are working in it. The obnoxious washing contraption is loud enough to keep even the dead away. When the room is quiet though, the curious energies come out to explore.

Recently, Shawn was working at the theater one afternoon. He was in the house and remembered something he needed to grab from the kitchen. Trying to manage his time efficiency, he took the shortcut through the wait station to get to the kitchen. As he rounded the corner, he saw a white mist hovering in the center of the dish room. He described it as not having a shape and that it looked more like a ball of swirling, white smoke.

In his mind, he tried to logically explain what the mist could be. The sighting occurred during the day, so the dishwashing equipment had not been used since the night before. Before he could come up with a possibility, the mist had dissolved.

As Shawn was telling me his experience, Robert interjected that he has actually seen this mist as well. Both men were surprised at that revelation because they had never compared stories.

With the dishwashing room being about ten feet from the lobby, I wonder if it is the same white mist that is seen moving through that area. Maybe. The only item to note is that the two mists are sized and shaped differently.

Weeks after I documented the experiences in this room, Shawn made mention of a former employee who passed away suddenly in the dish room. He was employed by the Harlequin and part of his job was to wash the dishes after shows. I don't know if he is associated with the white mist that both Shawn and Robert saw. If so, I hope he knows that he is always welcome to come visit his old stomping grounds.

Man in the Buffet Area

Directly off the kitchen is the buffet area. Once used for the dinner service, this space housed a salad bar, a soup area, a meat carving station, and a hot food serving center with one to two servers portioning meals to hungry patrons.

Now, it's simply an area where we can easily store and access commonly used props and costumes. It's in this area is where the gray headed man has been seen.

Buffet area.
Photo Credit: Cameron Kofoet

Sometimes when you are working hard on preparing for a show, you can easily get so absorbed in the tasks at hand that you forget to notice things out of the ordinary. That is exactly what happened to Robert one late afternoon in the fall of 2014.

Being the busy bee that he normally is, Robert was setting up the dining room for the show later that evening. Because it was a Thursday show, the planned attendance was lower than a weekend night, so the number of tables he had set up was less than normal. Working alone in the building, he had just finished the set up.

Knowing he had a number of tasks to finish before the theater doors opened, he decided he was going to finish everything in that area to avoid going back in later. As he made his way to the light booth to set the pre-show music, he thought he saw someone standing in the far corner of the buffet area out of the corner of his eye. Sure that he was alone, he looked toward the figure to see who it was.

There, standing about twenty feet in front of him, was a gray-haired man. He stood approximately Robert's height with unruly gray hair. Robert stopped dead in his tracks and stared. The man offered up a smile then disappeared. Robert stood looking at the now empty corner for a moment before carrying on with his task.

When experiencing paranormal activity, it can be heart-warming, startling, or downright frightening. I've noticed that when I'm experiencing activities, my mind is almost in overload. It's trying to accept what is physically being seen, heard or felt while generating thousands of questions on how this could be happening logically. I believe that is why so many people are paralyzed during the event.

In this case, Robert felt safe, so he was comfortable continuing with his professional duties. Every supernatural experience evokes a different reaction, primarily driven by the mind of the person experiencing it. If the mind assesses the situation as safe, a person does not flee in fear.

On the other hand, a mind that translates a threat will drive a person out of the closest exit. Robert regularly sees the gray haired man in the buffet area.

Maybe we will never know why, but Robert sees it as a wonderful gift. He is thrilled that the man comes for visits and feels comfortable sharing the space with him.

The Voice

Not all entities at the Harlequin are as pleasant as the gray-haired man. The meaner ones have different ways of chasing you away from them. In this incident, the spirit could not have been more clear.

One late Friday afternoon, Shawn was working alone in the theater setting up the house. There are quite a few tasks associated with readying the room for a show - from the table set up to program placement to vacuuming to general tidying up. Your mind gets in a "zone" and goes into routine mode. Most days, you don't hear anything going on around you because of your laser focus.

When Shawn is working on the set-up, he's usually playing music on his phone to sing along with while he works on his to dos. That is what makes this experience so impactful.

After finishing the diet up, Shawn was singing along with the music when he remembered that he needed to turn on the backstage lights. Nonchalantly, he walked through the house and had just reached the threshold of the buffet area when he heard a deep male voice.

"LEAVE!" it said.

The powerful voice was loud, clear and threatening.

Shawn didn't wait around to hear the voice again. He flipped the light switch, grabbed his things, and ran of the building.

Doppelgänger

The laundry area is situated off the kitchen at the far end. Before the theater discontinued the dinner service, this area was used to wash and steam linens. Now, it is used for costume laundry and storage.

The room is fairly neutral meaning there isn't a good or bad feeling associated with it. It's just there, if that makes sense. Experiences in this room have been fairly simple and non-threatening. In the past, only shadows have been seen moving though this room when the lights are off; however, a recent sighting changed all that.

In December of 2016, we were in the middle of the Christmas musical production, *Christmas Wishes*. Intermission for the show had just begun and I had gone backstage to discuss sound notes with Shawn.

Because all the lights in the kitchen area are on during shows, he and I were walking from backstage to the box office through the well illuminated kitchen. As we were passing the laundry area, I saw a man standing there with his face toward the corner wall. If you've seen *The Blair Witch Project*, that is exactly how this figure was standing. He was about my height with dark hair wearing baggy jeans and a dark grey sweater.

I literally stopped in my tracks, blinked, and it was gone. The confusion must have said it all on my face because Shawn's concern started immediately.

"What's wrong?" he said.

"Did you see him?" I asked.

"Who?" he responded.

"Robert," I said.

"Robert's working the bar," he said.

"But, I swear that I just….." I said.

Unnerved, he grabbed my arm and directed me to the lobby then the lounge. There was Robert, working at the bar. And he was wearing baggy jeans and a dark grey sweater. Confused, I just stared at him then looked back at Shawn.

Shawn is one of my very best friends. Believe me, he has no problem telling me when he thinks I've lost my mind. In fact, he's told me on several occasions. This time, he knew by the look on my face that I had seen something.

I still don't know why I saw the figure and he didn't. I don't know why it looked exactly like the back of Robert. And I certainly don't know why the Harlequin presents experiences that make you question your sanity. I do know that I saw that man standing there, and I'm positive it was Robert.

Was it a mash up of an alternative dimension? Was it an entity taking the shape of Robert to get my attention? I have no idea. My guess is that I will probably never know.

The kitchen at the Harlequin is a strange place. We have constant reports of all kinds of activity - pots and pans banging, children laughing, things falling, even reports of disembodied singing. When investigated, nothing is found out of place, and the room is always empty.

CHAPTER
6

House

While the stage is the most exciting part of the theater, the house a.k.a. dining room can range from highly energetic to super quiet. Some audiences feed the cast by cheering them on, clapping loudly, and singing along with the songs while other audiences remain quiet and reserved. Either way, the cast hits the stage with all the energy they can muster.

Filled with a minimum of twenty eight tables that all seat six, this is the spot where audiences enjoy all the live shows. The decor is simple chic with black walls, black tables, and silvery black chairs, matching all seasons and show themes. Patrons enter this room through the lobby; however, there is a second entrance from the lounge area.

When preparing for shows, this is the space used by the cast and crew to lay out costumes, brainstorm set design, rehearse choreography, create sound magic, and run lines or songs.

With a variety of activities going on, this room can be more active than the stage at times. At any time, you could be thrown into a paranormal experience. Voices, shadows, apparitions, moving objects, shadow figures, you name it, it's happened in this very room.

Man by the Board

Not all paranormal experiences are frightening. As a matter of fact, some can be enlightening even comforting. For me, the man by the board reminds me that even spirits enjoy a good show.

Since the summer of 2012, I have been the sound technician for all the musical productions. Never in a million years would I have ever thought I could do it, but when you have people that believe in you, the possibilities are endless. This time, Shawn and Seeley told me I could. Because they believed in me and trusted me, I refused to let them down.

I take the responsibility of sound very seriously because I know the importance of getting it right. It's exciting, rewarding, and most of all fun. There is never a dull moment and every performance is different from the soundboard. And as an added bonus, I have these incredibly cool mentors, Kyle Lassalle and

Mando Aussenac who have helped teach me everything I know.

To ensure the best quality experience for the cast and audience, the board is situated at the back of the house directly between the exit doors to the lounge and lobby. My location can be wonderful or terrible depending on the night, the weather, and the mood of people in the general area. When I say mood, I do mean mood. People are not always kind to those working hard to bring a show to life, but that is for another book at another time. All that aside, let it be known that I can handle almost anything that goes on as well as react to most unexpected situations.

The first time I ran sound, I was absolutely terrified. It's easier now, but I still get nervous before every show. Our shows run for approximately seven weeks with three performances per week. It was during my first run that I noticed a man watching over my shoulder. I couldn't look directly at him because I was fully focused on the stage and cast; however, I knew he was there.

With his gray, fuzzy hair, a white button-up shirt, and khaki pants, I could see him in my peripheral vision leaned up against the door frame from the lobby into the house. I was thrilled to have someone so close showing his appreciation for the show. Honestly, I didn't think anything of it. Just another patron enjoying one of our spectacular shows.

It wasn't until about three or four shows later that I began to realize that I see him every single run. Not every performance but at least one time throughout the run. I asked Robert who the guy was. He looked at me like I was crazy. That was the moment I thought here we go again.

The next show, I waited and waited until one night I finally saw him there in my peripheral vision. As I reached the perfect moment in the show where I could take my eyes off the stage and the board, I looked over at him. There was no one there. I wasn't surprised. Sad, yes. Surprised, no.

Recently, Brad and Barry Klinge came into the Harlequin to conduct a live investigation. Luckily, they let me participate. I felt like the dork of the group as I worked with them. They had all this cool, technical equipment; all I had was my cell phone, a stockpile of personal experiences, and an eagerness to prove that the Harlequin spirits really are there.

During the equipment set up, I shared my experience with the man by the board. They listened carefully and took note of what I was saying. Thinking I sounded like a crazy person, I eventually stopped talking. Not long after I finished, Brad shared with me that he too had seen this man many years ago in the exact same spot. Because of our similar experiences, he set up a green laser contraption in hopes to prove this spirit's existence to others.

How amazing was that? Brad not only believed me, he validated my experience by sharing that he had the exact same occurrence with the same man years ago. I was over the moon thankful that he shared it with me. Unfortunately, we didn't capture any evidence of the man that night, but Brad's validation confirmed my sanity.

The man by the board has come to a performance in every single run until this year. In the fall of 2016, the Harlequin produced an original show called *Lady Sings the Blues*. Sadly, he did not make an appearance at any of those performances. I hoped I would get to see him during the Christmas musical, but he was absent for that one too. I have to say that I miss his presence. He gave off such a loving and supportive energy. I don't know where he went, but I hope he found his happily ever after.

Native American Spirit

As Florence and I walked through the Harlequin discussing the history of the building, we stopped briefly in the lobby to chat with Robert. She referenced the history of the land that Fort Sam Houston sits on and the battles associated with it.

As she shard the brief history with Robert and me, it triggered a memory in her. Florence gathered her thoughts and began recanting the story.

Many times when shows are about to open, special guests are invited to previews of the show. You may have heard the term "soft opening" or "special showing." They are all different ways to say the same thing.

During the production of *The Rainmaker* in the seventies, Florence was coordinating the preview and invited her friend Felicia to see it.

On the night of the preview showing, Felicia arrived at the theater with her two kids. Florence greeted them with a warm and welcoming hug. Knowing that children usually want to be up close and that the audience size would be significantly smaller, Florence told the kids they were welcome to sit in the front row.

The group walked into the house ready to take their seats. Florence noticed the young boy's hesitancy as he whispered something in his mother's ear.

"What's wrong?" Florence asked.

"He doesn't like the man on the stage," Felicia said, then shrugged.

Florence looked up at the stage. Nothing was there except the set and props. Confused, she looked back to the young boy.

"Why don't you want to sit up front?" she asked.

"There is an Indian walking around on the stage talking to himself," he responded.

Because Florence has been told by mediums about the Native Americans in the building, she knew the boy was telling the truth.

"No problem at all. You can sit wherever you'd like," she told him.

The boy selected the table that was most comfortable for him and the family enjoyed the showing of the production. Luckily, the Native American man did not appear again that night.

Disappearing Patrons

Similar to the man by the board, there have been experiences of patrons sitting in the house that are there one minute and gone the next. In these reports, these phantoms were seen straight on not through peripheral vision. Could they be time slips? Residual hauntings? Ghosts just having fun with the living? I guess it could be anything. In our experience so far, all of these entities have been non-threatening.

A few years ago, Matthew Kjos, Shawn's youngest brother, volunteered at the Harlequin as the head of waitstaff. As a handsome and outgoing young man who was well-liked by the patrons, I would categorize him as a "cautious skeptic" who converted to "cautious believer." Initially, I think he believed we were all crazy until he started having creepy experiences of his own.

One night before opening, Matthew was prepping the wait station for dinner that night. Always moving at a hundred miles an hour, he was zipping in and out from the kitchen to the house to the wait station.

About ten minutes prior to the house opening, Matthew noticed a group of four soldiers sitting at a table. Thinking that

Shawn allowed them to enter early due to their military status, Matthew walked past the table, greeted the gentlemen, and told them that he would be with them momentarily. Without acknowledging him, they continued with their conversation. Realizing he was being ignored, Matthew walked through the curtains, breezing past Shawn who stood at the usher's table.

"I'll get to the soldiers in one sec. I have to run to the back," Matthew said.

"What soldiers?" Shawn said.

"The ones you let in early," Matthew said as he rushed past.

Shawn pulled the curtain back, looked into the theater then back at Matthew.

"What are you talking about? There's no one in the theater," Shawn said.

Matthew stopped, walked to Shawn, and looked back in the theater. There was no one there. Confused, Matthew shook his head and walked away.

Another night, Robert was cleaning up the house after a show. He would take a cart from table to table, pick up the dirty dishes, and take them to the dishwashing room to be washed.

During one of his trips back and forth, he stopped momentarily to assess the room, getting an idea of what was left to do. There, seated at one of the far tables, was a middle-aged woman with her head down looking sad and forlorn. He saw her for a moment before she disappeared right before his eyes. Because she was only seen that one time, I'm hoping she was able to move on.

The Black Shadow

Several of our Harlequin family members are quite sensitive; however, there are two that the rest of us watch - Johnny, our Earth angel and Ashton, my daughter. Both of them are somehow able to sense energy long before the rest of us realize a presence is there. It can be a blessing for the rest of us, but it's sometimes a curse for the two of them. On some occasions, they will have an experience and the rest of us will miss it completely. One such occasion happened during a rehearsal for the 2015 summer show, *Cocktail Hour*.

Johnny, an extremely gifted and amazing dancer, takes great pride in sharing his graceful brilliance with his family at the theater. Many performers found their dancing feet under the tutelage of our Johnny Angel. Karson Kelley, Sarah Peters, Seeley Stephens, Ashton Folsom, Katie Molina, Lauren Silva, Garrett Scot Henry, Melissa Dean, and Samantha Eberle are just a few.

This particular rehearsal, Johnny was working with Ashton on choreography. During one of the moves and at the exact same time, both sensed something afoot and looked out the house door into the lobby. There stood a tall black shadow figure outlined by a pulsing, black mist. The figure moved from the stairs area disappearing into the lounge.

What made this figure different from others seen in the past was the mist surrounding it. Ashton described it as being like an aura or smoke around a person. She said the experience happened quickly and took them both completely off guard.

Strangely, she walked away from it as a wonderful validation of her gift because both, she and Johnny saw the entity at the exact same time.

Small Black Mass

Recently, the Harlequin presented a production of *The Birds*. While the content of the play itself is dark and eerie, the cast was exposed to something even creepier during rehearsals. The week before opening of any show is known as "tech week." It tends to be quite hectic with last minute costume changes, set finalization, lighting design edits, and the important dress rehearsals. This tech week was no difference than any other until two nights before opening.

With the cast members on stage, running lines, it was a normal evening. Suddenly, Robert saw something moving out of the corner of his eye. He turned quickly and his eyes caught a small black mass peeking out of the wait station into the house at the back of the theater. When I asked Robert to describe the entity, he indicated that it was about his height which is approximately 5 feet 9 inches. He said that the black shadow gave the impression that it wanted to watch the rehearsal but didn't want to be seen.

Every time, Robert looked at it, the shadow would pull back into the wait station. Frustrated, he began to watch the entity from his peripheral vision. It moved back and forth between the wait station and the house entrance from the lobby. This continued through the entire first act. He did his best watch the entity without distracting the cast. Finally, he made one last attempt to look directly at it. It quickly moved into the wait station again.

Finally, they took a break. Wanting to validate what he was seeing, he asked the cast to watch that area.

One by one, each of the cast members saw the shadow. Stunned, they looked at each other trying to determine what to do. Because it gave no indication of a threat and they had quite a bit of rehearsing to get though, they decided to push forward and ignore it.

After the cast refocused on the rehearsal, it was not seen a again until rehearsals started for the next play when it appeared once again.

Invisible Force

Whether you are Madonna performing to an arena size audience, Idina Menzel performing on a Broadway stage, or a volunteer performer in a community theater, you are in the entertainment business.

It doesn't matter if you are on stage or backstage. You could be the set designer, costumer, writer, director, stage manager, sound technician, lighting technician, or a stage hand fulfilling one the billion tasks required to bring a production to life. No matter what your job is, this career choice is a fun and exciting path to follow. You will meet some of the most interesting and incredibly talented people that walk the Earth. Glitz and glamour at its finest.

It's no secret that this industry can be cut-throat, catty, narcissistic, divisive, even manipulative, but it can also be supportive, enlightening, uplifting, rewarding, even life changing. If your really lucky, you will find yourself surrounded by an incredible family who will celebrate your wins, catch you when you fall, and hold you up when you aren't strong enough to do it for yourself.

At the Harlequin, that is what we are - a family. This place is uniquely wonderful and our family is constantly growing. Our staple cast and crew are constantly being told by every new performer that works with us that we are unlike any theater they have ever performed at.

We offer a warm, inviting, and supportive environment whose goal is to shine light into the world through love and inclusion. We believe in giving opportunities, taking risks, and being the positive light that allows people to overcome obstacles by pushing them past any self-imposed hurdle put in their way. Many theaters could learn a lot from this approach.

One of the best things about the Harlequin family is that we adhere to a fun yet important rule: work hard, play hard. After intense rehearsals or nights, we are always looking for ways to lighten the mood and make each other laugh. Life is more fun with a smile on your face.

After a particularly intense show one evening in the summer of 2013, the theater had cleared out with the exception of Robert and Shawn. Because of some unexplained bumps and bangs earlier in the day, they worked together to clean up the dining room and bar area.

Typically, one of the two would open the wall partition between the buffet area and the dining room, but this night they kept it shut. There was no risk because the partition has a door allowing easy access to the house.

After completing the clean-up, they agreed to divide and conquer the last set of the tasks. Robert made his way to the box office to finish the books while Shawn headed backstage to close everything down. He locked the doors, turned off the lights, and did his final sweep of the area before making his way toward the house.

As you walk past the light booth, there's a light switch that turns off the lights in the tech area. Shawn had just reached the light switch and was lifting his hand to flip the switch when he heard the wall partition door move. He stopped mid-flip and looked toward it as it began to close on its own. Irritated because it had been a long night and he thought Robert was messing with him, he impatiently called out.

"Hello?" Shawn asked.

As soon as the word left Shawn's mouth, the door stopped instantly.

No response.

After a beat, it slowly began to open in the opposite direction. Frustrated and unamused, Shawn went to the door yanking it opening expecting to find Robert.

No one was there.

He rushed out of the house and stormed into the box office. There sat Robert diligently working on the books. Shawn quickly looked back at the house then back to Robert.

"What's wrong?" Robert asked.

Shawn didn't bother responding. He grabbed his bag and left the building immediately.

Balls of Light

This is not a particular story but more of a specific phenomena - balls of light. I'm not talking about the balls of light that we have debunked such as headlights, watch reflections, phones, and the like. What I'm referring to are the floating balls of light that have no light source. They just appear out of no where.

During *London Calling*, we caught a picture of a green one. I've chosen not to share the photo because skeptics would debunk it in a second. But seeing it with your own eyes? Well, that is not as easily dismissed.

I don't have any other proof than to say they're real and are making regular appearances at the Harlequin.

CHAPTER

7

Stage

Ah, the stage. The glorious stage. The heart of the theater. The center of the action. The source of the energy. The reason every person that walks in this building is here. At approximately forty feet wide and twenty-five feet deep, it's been an apartment in New York, a flat in London, a plantation in Louisiana, a winter wonderland, a haunted house, a secret garden, and hundreds of other scenes. One thing it rarely is - quiet.

From moving objects to strange mists to shadow figures, this stage has seen its share of paranormal activities. The entities have even been known to watch performers on stage from the wings. As frightening as this stage can be, each of the Harlequin's cast and crew gladly chooses to face their fears and accept any experience that may come every time they step on this platform. Sometimes, performing in front of live audience is less terrifying than some the things roaming around backstage.

There are dozens upon dozens of strange occurrences and unexplained events in this particular area. While I've captured a few incidents in this book, there are many more where these came from.

Lurking in the Back

My husband and I learned a long time ago how sensitive Ashton is. From the moment she started talking to "the people" at about three until now, she's always seen things that aren't always visible to others. At times, she is like a magnet to entities. Ashton isn't exactly thrilled about her gift, but she does her best to manage it.

For a few years, she was unknowingly the person that Shawn and I watched to see if something is there. Our theory has been if Ashton's good, everyone's good.

Everyone has their quirks. Ashton's is protecting her ears. When she senses something nearby, she subconsciously lifts her hands to cover her ears. I don't know if she is trying to block out sound or if it is just her personal reaction to energies. I've asked her but even she doesn't know. Most of us at the theater know to watch Ashton. If she covers her ears, make like Jack Sparrow and "keep a sharp eye."

It was the Spring of 2013 and the cast was in rehearsals for *Broadway Divas,* which would be Ashton's first main stage show.

Because she was young and performing with five other powerhouse ladies, Shawn had her come to the theater one night to work with her on the blocking for one of her songs. Ashton and I greeted Shawn outside and the three of us made our way into the theater. Because we were the only people there, the environment was prime opportunity for learning.

Standing in front of the stage, Shawn explained to Ashton that he wanted her to enter from the far back of the stage with the music and slowly work her way to the front while dragging a chair with her right hand. Because she was wearing a headset microphone, her left hand was the only one free.

Shawn and I talked while Ashton made her way backstage, grabbed her chair and went to her place on stage.

"You ready?" he asked her.

"Yep," she said.

I headed back to the sound board and started the music. She performed her song, then she and Shawn talked about modifications. After talking through it, they agreed to do it again. Ashton walked back to her spot, looking confident and ready to begin.

Suddenly, I watched her face change from a smile to pure fear followed by her left hand reaching to cover her left ear. Because this was her first main stage show, Shawn was still learning about her sensitivities. He turned and looked at me with his "what the hell is going on" face. Knowing something was there and she could sense it, I tried to take her mind off of it.

"Are you okay?" I asked her.

"Yes. Please turn on the music," she said.

"Are you sure?" Shawn said.

"Yes," she responded.

I started the music and walked to Shawn. Ashton started the performance from the back and moved quickly to her spot in at the front of the stage. Shawn looked at me then back to her. I whispered to him that I would explain later.

After she finished, Shawn walked to the stage and expressed how well the modifications looked. Still uneasy, she smiled and thanked him.

"Do you need to run it again?" he asked.

"No, I'm good," she responded.

She jumped off the front of the stage and ran to the lobby for a drink of water. Shawn then walked to me looking for an explanation for what just happened. I explained her sensitivity and how she reacts to energies. He completely understood. That was the moment Shawn began watching Ashton to see if there was something he needed to be concerned with at the theater.

That night, the backstage entity only made her aware of its

presence. It did not show itself. The gift from that night is Shawn and Ashton's relationship. He has always been extremely protective of Ashton, but now, he watches her like a hawk. If she feels threatened or senses something bad, he listens and trusts her instinct. He takes whatever action necessary to take her attention away from it even if that means they run out to Starbucks for a hot beverage.

Thrown Off Stage

On many occasions, several people at the Harlequin have witnessed objects moving on their own. Although the locations of these activities vary, they have been reported to occur all over the theater, but some of the most notable reports come from the stage. More times than not, movement like this is explained away. Maybe the person witnessing it was tired or their eyes were playing tricks on them. There are times, however, when there is no denying it.

These true unexplainable events occurred regardless of what was happening - during rehearsals, production set up, even during live shows. Some of the most legendary events happen in the span of a few seconds yet they leave the most memorable impression.

Almost seven years ago, a cast of six was performing in a live musical production. Three men and three women energetically delivered a fifties revue of fifty to sixty songs strung together to entertain the Harlequin audiences.

After one set of songs, the stage would go to a blackout for about three to four seconds to prepare for the next set of songs. This blackout leaves a small amount of light on the stage to allow the performers to navigate the stage safely and efficiently.

During a particular performance, I was watching from the director's table at the back of the house. The girls had just finished their beautiful trio performance where each one sat on one of three strategically placed metal swivel stools. The lights went down and the girls moved the stools to their regular resting spot on stage left. We could hear their footsteps as they made their way backstage to change for the next number.

Just as the music was going to start or the next number, a loud crash came from the stage left side of the stage. I knew it was one of the metal stools. Fearing that one of cast members had fallen and was hurt, I immediately ran to the side of the stage. Luckily, the only thing on the floor was a broken metal stool.

Based on where I found it, it had been thrown off the stage and was now scattered across the theater floor. Nervously, I collected the pieces of the stool, thankful that no one was hurt, then breathed a deep sighed of relief.

I'm sure the skeptics out there are assuming that one of the girls sat the stool down haphazardly and it simply fell over. As a cautious skeptic, I questioned the same thing. Let me explain why I know it wasn't one of the girls.

During the show, the stools had a designated location which was located approximately seven feet from the side of the stage. Even if the stool had tipped over, it still wasn't tall enough to fall off the stage. The only way for it to have fallen to the floor would have been for it to have been pushed or thrown off. Because the girls were almost off stage when the stool fell, I know they couldn't have pushed it and the guys weren't on the stage yet.

To this day, the reason for the event is still unknown.

Ready for a Close Up

Every once in awhile, paranormal experiences occur around us and we are oblivious to them. One such time, this happened to one of the lead characters in front of a live audience. She was the closest person to the unexplained activity and had no idea it was happening. I happened to be in the audience for this performance and even I didn't see the activity.

During a performance of *Dial M for Murder*, there are a few scenes where some of the characters are briefly on stage alone. It's a fascinating murder mystery and the characters command your attention the entire performance.

This night, the play was flowing at a perfect pace and Jenn Harris, one of the leads, was on stage waiting for her male counterpart to join her.

In the light booth, Robert's eye was pulled to the black curtain on stage left. At the same time, Shawn was in the audience and his eye was pulled to the same black curtain.

While the audience listened to Jenn deliver her lines, watching carefully for foreshadowing clues as the story unfolds, Shawn and Robert saw the curtain begin to open. It opened far enough for a human to walk out of it, yet no one came though.

Immediately, Robert ran around backstage to tell the cast not to mess with or enter via that curtain. When he got to the back, they were all near the dressing room door. No one was even remotely near the curtain.

When Robert returned to the light booth, the curtain had closed. After the show, he checked with Shawn and me to see if we happened to witness the same event. I shook my head no, but Shawn said he did. He thought it was a cast member messing with the curtain. Robert shared with him where the cast was backstage. We still have no idea what was opening that curtain.

Floating Microphone

I may say it multiple times, but I can't express enough how powerfully fifties music affects the energies of the Harlequin. This incident occurred during the same run as the floating stools. It was during one of the rehearsals and the cast was in the dining room.

After running the first act, they decided to stop for a few minutes to rest before starting act two. Typically during the rest, the cast will check their phones, grab a drink, eat a snack, or just sit around talking.

Two off the cast members, Shawn and Kylee Skye Lynn, happened to be talking when Kylee noticed something didn't look right on stage. Noticing her confused look, Shawn shifted his gaze to where Kylee was looking.

They both were watching when one of the microphones lifted out of the mic stand and began floating across the stage. Within seconds, it dropped to the ground. They both just stood there stunned.

"Oh my God. Did you see that?" Kylee screamed.

Shawn nodded speechless.

They both turned around to see if anyone else had witnessed this incredible event. The director and one of the other cast members were in the room but weren't looking at the stage. They were both angry that they had missed it.

Crazy Saloon Doors

During the rehearsals for shows, the cast will run through the songs in order to ensure choreography is clean, spacing is even, and blocking is understood. Blocking is a theatrical term that covers the stage - where you enter, where you exit, and where you go while you are on stage. Blocking is usually focused on last after the choreography is finished and any show modifications have been completed.

Late in 2011, the Harlequin produced a high energy country show. With a set designed to look like a location in an old ghost town, it came complete with a a horse saddle station, a simple wood deck, and a rustic saloon with the well known saloon doors. The cast was excited and the patrons were already buying tickets for the show. Choreography was done and the cast was working through the blocking.

All six of the cast members had gone to separate places on the stage to write down where they were entering and exiting. As they finished, a few of them noticed the director watching the saloon doors. They turned to look.

The saloon doors were slowly opening as though someone was walking through them to enter the stage. Then, they began to close as though the entry was complete. With the entire cast was on stage and the director in the dining room, no one could have been near the doors.

Flying Soup Lid

Dress rehearsals are usually held for several days occurring every day up to opening night. Translated into common language, a dress rehearsal is an end to end run through of the entire show in costume, hair and make-up.

That said, make-up can be expensive, so there are times where a decision is made to run with just costume and hair.

I know, I know. You are thinking why hair? Well, the answer is simple. Many performers wear wigs. If they go without one, their real hair is teased, curled, or one of many things to make sure it looks good onstage.

When a performer changes in and out of costumes, they have no idea how it will affect their hair. Doing a dress rehearsal in costume helps identify any potential hair issues, so they can be resolved before a live performance. Believe me, I have seen hair disasters. They are not cute and the performers are not happy. Happy performer equals happy show.

We were working through one of the last rehearsals for the 2014 fall show, *Where The Boys Are*.

In 2014, the Harlequin was still serving dinner, so Robert worked diligently to ensure the buffet area was ready for the opening night. As a matter of fact, the entire theater was in perfect order. The only action item remaining was to run through a few dress rehearsals.

That night, the cast had just completed one of them and was backstage changing out of their costumes and hair.

One by one, they made their way out to the house for Shawn to share "show notes" with them. Show notes are little things that need to be fixed prior to the show opening. At this point, most of the girls were seated around talking and waiting for the last girl to come out, Nicki Martinez.

Within a minute or so, we heard Nicki yelling that she was on her way. As she came around the light booth and entered the buffet area, the lid from the soup pot flew off crashing to the buffet floor with loud bang. Finally, it bounced onto the carpeted floor of the house. The look on her face morphed from complete confusion to pure terror. She screamed.

"Oh my God. Did you guys see that?" she screamed.

None of us had. All we saw was Nicki standing about ten feet from the soup pot and the lid on the carpet. We all checked on Nicki while Robert ran over to see what could have caused the soup lid to fly off. He found absolutely no reason for it.

Moving Vase

Before a show one afternoon, Robert was working alone in the house preparing the tables for dinner. He completed the set-up of the first row and was moving into the second row when he heard something move onstage. It sounded like something sliding across a table. Not knowing where the source of the noise was, he looked up at the stage and watched for a few moments.

Nothing.

He had just gone back to work on the second row set-up when he heard it again.

Inquisitively, he scanned the stage slowly looking for potential culprits and settled his eyes on a vase sitting on the side table. It was really the only item on the stage that could have made a noise similar to what he was hearing. Suddenly, the vase slid about four inches across the side table by itself.

Looking for a logical explanation, he stepped up on the stage to find the cause of the noise. The table was stable and the surrounding area was clear of anything that could have fallen against the table causing the vase to move. Perplexed, he scratched his head and went about his tasks.

"Just don't break anything," he said quickly to the air.

CHAPTER
8

Backstage

Believe it or not, the backstage of the Harlequin is one of the most haunted areas of the theater. I can say this confidently and undoubtedly because I personally have experienced more occurrences that I can count back there including the most frightening experience I've ever had in my entire life.

Unfortunately, I'm not alone. Seven out of ten people that have spent a significant amount of time backstage have their own stories to tell. Heck, I could have filled this chapter with just my own experiences, but I thought it wouldn't be fair to the spirits to only share what I've seen.

From heavy breathing to balls of light to shadow figures to strange smells to moving objects, the backstage has more stories that you can imagine. While most of these accounts are personal experiences, paranormal investigators have captured video evidence of one report.

The Klinge Brothers love investigating The Harlequin because the evidence they have captured in the past is solid.

In one of their first investigations at the Harlequin, they were video recording backstage in the dressing room. The camera happened to be focused on one of the chairs. While they were talking, the chair moved several inches by itself. They have the captured video footage in their records and have shared it on a variety of media outlets.

There are so many stories out there. The following accounts are personal experiences that are being shared for the first time in this book.

A Woman's Sigh

Right before an actor goes onstage, they stand in what we call the wings. This is the place where the actors can watch or listen to the action on the stage while preparing themselves to go live. Here they might be reviewing lines, quietly conducting a vocal warm up, guzzling a glass of water, applying last looks, or simple just pumping each other up for their scenes.

My personal favorite routine belongs to Seeley Stephens and Sarah Peters. They used to do what they called "energy hops." The two girls would stand facing each other, jump up and down while whispering energy, energy, energy. It was fabulously entertaining for me to watch and gave me a jolt of electricity that lasted all night long. I miss their energy together and love them both dearly.

In 2010, I was cast in a Harlequin production called *God's Favorite* with Sarah. No matter what, Sarah always has and always will keep my energy levels high with her beautiful smile, incredible voice, and Pantene hair. Sarah was cast as my daughter in this show and from that point on became my daughter in life.

During this same production, I also met a wonderful new friend named Lisa Valle. She and I enjoyed performing together and talked all the time especially in the wings before we were to go onstage.

One particular night, Lisa and I were waiting in the wings for our cues to go onstage. I was standing near the entry door ready to walk on and Lisa was seated on the bench approximately three feet from me.

Based on the lines being delivered on stage, I knew my cue was coming in the next thirty seconds. Suddenly, I heard a loud female sigh coming from right beside me. Thinking that Lisa had moved up beside me for some reason, I looked over toward her. She was still sitting on the bench, but she was looking back at me strangely. Before I could say anything, she spoke.

"I heard that too," she whispered.

I'm pretty sure I ran on stage that night and I don't think either of us waited for a cue.

The Shadow Man

On a regular basis, we see what is commonly known as a shadow person backstage. Always seen as a tall, black human-shaped shadow with little to no detail, he comes with a strong sense of foreboding.

During shows, he can often be seen looking at you from the opposite side of the stage. Many of the shadow man appearances have occurred during live shows making it nearly impossible to photograph. Additionally, the witnesses to these entities are acting as stage managers at the time of the event, so they are in the middle of a job.

It's almost as if the shadow knows that these people can't go anywhere or do anything. While we have received numerous reports of these figures, we only have one photo that captures a slight glimpse of what we see.

One thing to note is that theater people are extremely dedicated to their craft. If the devil himself approached them during a show, they may be startled but the show must go on. They would probably find a way to have the devil hold props until the show ends. After the curtain closes, they will flee like a screaming banshee.

During a 2016 production of *The Birds*, Michael Zaiontz was playing a dual role. Offstage, he was the stage manager while onstage, he played the crazy neighbor. Because his powerful performance was only in one act of the show, he was able to focus fully on the stage management aspect the rest of the show.

It wasn't long after the show began live productions that Michael started to see the shadow figure watching him. If Michael was setting up props on stage right, it would peek out from behind the curtains on stage left. If he was on stage left, it would pop out from behind the wood panels on stage right. It never came close to him, but the shadow knew that Michael was aware of its presence.

Michael is one of the nicest and most genuine people I know. Having this entity mess with him angered me. I guess it's my motherly instinct.

During this same production, another strange phenomenon occurred. Footsteps could be heard walking toward the curtain as if to open it. Good news is the curtain never opened. Bad news is that we have no idea where they went. Were the footsteps and the shadow from the same entity?

He's Watching

Another Harlequin production that had a high number of shadow man sightings was *Doo Wop City* in the summer of 2014. The cast had four guys and one girl, Seeley. Ashton was working backstage as the stage manager and Seeley's dresser. Because Ashton was backstage alone during most of the show, she had the highest potential to see this entity. While the run started out quietly, it wasn't long before the dark figure started to make its presence known.

The first sighting happened the second weekend of the show. Ashton was waiting with Seeley's clothes on stage left to help her change into her next costume. As she waited, she was overcome by an intense feeling of being watched. Fighting the urge to cover her ears, she tried to take her mind off her senses by looking around at the lights on the opposite side of the stage.

Without thinking, something caught her eye directly across from her. As her eyes adjusted, she could see it standing there staring back at her.

Ashton couldn't see the entity's eyes, but she could feel them burning into her. She looked away and tried to avoid seeing it. After what felt like an eternity, the song ended and Seeley exited for her change. Focusing on the change distracted Ashton and the shadow man disappeared.

Unfortunately, the sightings continued and this shadow followed Ashton around the entire run. To protect herself, she wore her cross necklace and said The Lord's Prayer regularly throughout the shows. While these protection tools did not stop the entity from showing itself to her, it did not touch her or even get close to her.

The tools gave her the strength to fight for her personal space and the courage to return night after night.

My Encounter

This was not my first encounter with a shadow figure, but it was my first time seeing one at the Harlequin. I was working as the stage manager and dresser in a 2011 musical revue. With a cast of six that needs props and quick changes throughout a show, the stage manager responsibilities can be overwhelming. Strong multitasking abilities are the minimum strengths you could offer. When focused on this many things at once, I allowed myself to be consumed by all the production tasks in front of me and escaped everything else going on in the world.

As the run progressed, I became better and better at knowing where I needed to be, what needed to be done, and who I needed to help. With that, I was able to relax and take a few moments to breathe here and there. Looking back, I should have kept myself wrapped up in the juggling of props and people.

One night, I had just finished hanging Sarah, Kylee, and Seeley's clothes and was standing on the ramp facing across the back of the stage. Because of the way it was built, I could see the whole way across to the other side of the stage.

After taking a moment to rest, I thought I saw something move on the opposite side of the stage. I lifted my head and fully focused in the area. Dim lights provide enough illumination for the cast to maneuver in the back during a show.

Suddenly, I noticed a large black shadow that appeared to be facing me. Neither of us moved. When I realized that the entire cast was onstage, my whole body filled with fear. Who was that? What was that? Before I could process what I was seeing, the girls walked off stage. I didn't want to scare them, so I kept my mouth shut, refocusing myself on helping them with their dresses.

After that night, I saw the shadow several times. There is no rhyme nor reason as to why it appears leaving the witness (me) confused and frightened.

What Do You Want

In addition to Ashton and Johnny, Florence has the ability to sense and feel the presence of a spirit; however, she doesn't see them with her eyes. Many times, sensitive individuals can sense the gender, age range, even the intention of the energies. Everyone has this ability built into their core, but some people chose to suppress it. Calm down, it's okay. I'm not mad at anyone for choosing to ignore it. You are your own person and you have to choose what is right for the path you are walking.

When Florence worked at the Harlequin, she did her best to stay in her space which usually did not take her much farther than the box office. This kept her fully focused on the work she needed to get done and allowed the spirits to roam freely throughout the rest of the theater.

Because Florence is an incredibly warm-hearted and caring individual, she treats every soul with kindness and respect. Her opinion is that these spirits have just as much right to be there as she does.

One afternoon as she diligently worked preparing for an evening show, she remembered that she needed to grab something from backstage. She made her way through the house and across the technical area backstage with no issues. As she got to the ramp that leads to the back of the stage, the hair on the back of her neck began to rise. Her senses began to tingle and her guard immediately went up. Cautiously, she pressed forward.

When Florence reached the top of the incline, her internal safety alarm was going off like a Texas tornado siren screaming for people to take cover. She stopped in her tracks. The thick energy was overwhelming. It was the presence backstage that she had only heard about.

Now, she could feel him trying to intimidate her with his cold, unfriendly attitude. Although he uttered no words, she unquestionably received the impression he was sending, "What do you want?"

Florence took a moment to gather her courage and spoke confidently out loud.

"I'm just here to grab something I forgot. It will only take a minute," she said.

As soon as the words left her mouth, the energy disappeared. She quickly gathered the items she had come to retrieve and made her way back to the box office with no further incident.

Shadow Man Caught

Because Robert is either in the light booth or onstage for every show, he sees this shadow person regularly. His vantage point is slightly different because he can see it from the light booth. Like everyone else, Robert has only ever seen one at a time, so we have yet to determine if there is just one or if there are multiple shadow people. Recounting some of his experiences with me, he seemed apprehensive to discuss them.

"It just stands and watches through eyes no one can see," Robert said.

Curious, I asked him where he sees the shadow figure. He said that he has seen it in multiple places around the theater. From the light booth, he can see it in the wings.

Knowing his sensitivity to spirits, I asked him how it makes him feel.

"It exudes terror," he said. "I feel like it is intentionally trying to intimidate and frighten anyone that sees it."

The best thing all of us can hope for is that we avoid it

completely.

Some time ago, this picture was taken at the theater during an investigation. Although it captured two strange things, the shadow person is what sent shivers down our spines. This is him - the exact entity that so many of us have seen in this theater. Just looking at the picture is terrifying because I have seen this entity with my own eyes.

 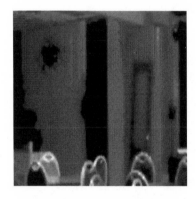

A snapshot of what we believe to be the shadow man that lurks backstage. Photo Credit: Robert Olivas

Yes, there is something else in that picture beyond the shadow figure. Your eyes aren't deceiving you. There's a white mist. While I can't explain it because I wasn't there when the picture was taken, I will say that it looks similar to the mists seen throughout the building by numerous witnesses including me.

Due to its location on the stage, there is a possibility that someone was testing hazers for an upcoming show. There is also a billion to one shot that we captured not one but two supernatural occurrences in the same photo. With this location, you never know what is going to or where it is going to pop up.

Sticky Mist

As I said previously, Johnny is one of our most sensitive individuals at the theater. Typically, he can tell you what the energy is like before he even walks into the building. If it's too bad, he won't even enter.

Unfortunately on this occasion, Johnny was already in the building. As we spoke about it, he shivered and said that this was the most frightening experience that he had at the theater to date.

During one of our fifties shows, Johnny happened to be the last person left backstage in the dressing room. After gathering his things and making sure all the ladies' styling tools were cooled down, he began to move toward the light booth, switching lights off as he went.

As he walked across the back of the stage and reached the ramp on stage right, he was hit with an sudden change in the environment. It was clammy and humid with a strong musty odor. Knowing this meant something was manifesting, Johnny moved quickly down the ramp toward the buffet area. His mission was to get out of that space before whatever was around made its appearance.

Just as he passed the door to the light booth, he could feel an aggressive, masculine energy approaching. Before he could react, he was surrounded by a thick, white mist. He described it as an ectoplasmic cigarette smoke that swirled around, completely covering him. Johnny swatted at it trying to get it to dissipate, but it stuck to him like a thick, gooey substance. His senses went into overdrive and he screamed.

Meanwhile, Shawn was in the lounge chatting with the another director when the sounds of Johnny's screams reached the front of the building. Frightened, Shawn went running backstage to help.

By the time Shawn got to him, the mist had dissipated, but Johnny could still feel the goo embracing him. Frightened and out of breath, he said to Shawn "I feel like my whole aura was hijacked."

After Shawn led him into the lounge and sat him on a chair, Johnny took a few moments to gather himself. Mustering up as much courage as he could, Johnny had a firm conversation with the spirits about jumping him and told them in no uncertain terms to never let it happen again.

It is never okay for a spirit to force itself upon you or anyone. You need to claim your space and set boundaries. If you don't take precautions to protect yourself, you are jeopardizing your life and your energy. If nothing else, envision yourself in a bubble of white light and always feel free to say The Lord's Prayer or whatever prayer of empowerment you find most relevant.

Scratched by the Ramp

When the children's program was active, some of the older kids would work backstage during main stage shows. This allowed them to appreciate the work that goes into the entire production not just the onstage performance. Honestly, the best kids to work with are the kids that put in time back there. They are good kids, hard workers, and end up being the least entitled and most humble.

One of the older kids at the time was Yleana Wooten. A beautiful, talented, and brilliant performer, Yleana owned the stage every time she took it. Today, she's just starting her adult life, but her bright star has not dimmed. She continues to grow and become more incredible to watch.

During one of the main stage shows in 2009-2010 season, she was resting backstage during a break in the live show. She chose to lay down over by the ramp area backstage because that was the quietest place she could find.

Stage right ramp area where scratches are regularly received.

Just as she started to get comfortable, she felt a pressure on her neck. Annoyed thinking it was someone messing with her, she sat up and looked around, ready to give them a piece of her mind. She whipped her head around only to find that she was alone.

Thinking she must have imagined it, she went back to resting. Within a few minutes, she felt it again, except this time, it was a more forceful pressure. It felt like a hand was pressing down on the back of her neck. Again, she sat up and visually scanned the area. No one.

Slightly unnerved but wanting to get as much rest as she could, she leaned back and closed her eyes. Before her head was down, she felt something sharply scratch the back of her neck. She jumped up screaming and ran into the bathroom backstage. When she looked in the mirror, she could see a long bright red scratch mark going down the back of her neck.

Twin Scratches

Conversations with witnesses often uncovered similar yet chilling accounts of the same type of experience. Scratches seem to be a regular occurrence backstage and specifically on stage right.

Recently Katie Molina, one of the most talented ladies I know and one of our Harlequin stars, was over at my house for a visit. We were catching up and talking about the progress of this book. She stopped for a moment to ponder a thought then began to recount an experience that she had had. Katie had no more than started the recollection when Ashton jumped in. "I remember that night. I forgot all about it."

We've all experienced so many things at the Harlequin. It's

almost like our brain gets used to it, and we forget. I'm so thankful that Katie and Ashton remembered this one.

During rehearsals for the 2015 summer show *Cocktail Hour*, the cast was working through choreography. Ashton was waiting in the wings on stage right with Garrett, her incredibly talented and handsome show partner.

Suddenly, Ashton felt a burning on her stomach. She attempted to ignore it, but the stinging wouldn't ease. Worried that she might be bleeding, she glanced at her stomach. There were three scratch marks. No blood, but a the skin was broken.

Knowing that they would still be dancing for a few more hours, she desperately tried to ignore her fear. Luckily, Garrett was nearby, and he could sense her nervousness.

Because he and Ashton have an amazing friendship and Garrett is one of the sweetest humans on the planet, he knew exactly what to do. In one swift move, he spun her onstage for the next number, immediately distracting her.

Katie came off stage at the same time. As she stood stage right waiting for her cue, she felt something strange scrape across her stomach. Before she could look, she heard her cue, stepped on stage, and finished the number.

Still feeling a burning sensation, she lifted her shirt slightly and gasped when she saw three long scratches across her abdomen. Hearing her reaction, Seeley and Shawn went to her.

Meanwhile, Ashton and Garrett were chatting nearby when they saw Katie showing something on her stomach. Curious, they approached. It wasn't until she saw Katie's scratches that Ashton realized this was a problem.

"Oh my God, Katie. I have those same scratches," Ashton said, lifting her shirt to reveal three matching scratches in the exact same position on her stomach.

After the revelation of those scratching experiences, I wonder how many more accounts exist that I haven't heard about.

It's frightening to know that these entities can touch even harm us if they choose to. I have to keep remembering that maybe they aren't trying to harm. What if they are just trying to get our attention? What if their actions are part of a message that we aren't understanding? Hell, what if they are trying to protect us from something else?

Rose Perfume

Spirits can reach out to us in many different ways. Some of them can be heard, some can be seen, and some send their messages through scent. Several of the Harlequin spirits have started communicating with us via smell. Three of the most common scents that have been reported are rose perfume, cigarettes, and a sulfur-like odor. The latter two have been experienced in multiple places throughout the theater while the rose perfume lingers in one small area. Because this aroma just started surfacing in March of 2016, it's possible that it is associated with someone we may know in particular.

In the spring of 2016, the Harlequin presented one of its edgiest yet most brilliant shows to date, *London Calling*. Larger than normal with twelve cast members, we had to create a few makeshift dressing stations to accommodate the sizable cast. One of these improvised stations was located in the back corner of backstage left. Because Shawn was directing and performing in the show, he chose to use this station because of its proximity to the stage.

Backstage left.
Photo Credit: Cameron Kofoet

One night, Shawn was talking with another one of our amazing choreographers, Laura Anglin before they took the stage. All of the sudden, a powerful scent of rose perfume surrounded them. Thinking it was a fluke, they ignored it and went on stage. After returning to change clothes for the next number, Shawn noticed the scent was gone. Before moving back onstage, Laura returned and noticed the smell had disappeared also.

Throughout the run, the scent was fairly prominent. While it wasn't present every night, it was frequent enough that people recognized it. There was no indication as to why it would appear and disappear randomly. Since *London Calling*, no one has dressed at that station so the reports of rose perfume smells have dropped.

No one at the theater knows where this aroma could have come from nor do they know anyone associated with the scent.

Many times, we find out about word, color, smell, or other associations by talking with each other. It's then that the light bulbs go off and we figure out the association. To date, we haven't discovered the correlation to the rose perfume. The only remote connection is that Laura's mom's name is Rose, but I think that we might be reaching on that one.

Maybe it belongs to a patron of the Harlequin? Or an old performer? Or the relative of a performer? Either way, the scent just started in March of 2016. We will uncover it sometime when we least expect it.

The Presence

People regularly ask me what my most frightening paranormal experience has been. Strangely, I'd describe most of my experiences as curious verses scary - with the exception of one.

In 2013, the Harlequin presented the stage play, *The Bad Seed*. Excellent show to open up the fall season as the content was creepy and Halloween was only a few weeks away. I was lucky enough to be cast in the show with Johnny, Samantha and several of my friends whom I love dearly. Backstage antics were almost as entertaining as the onstage performances. After the performances, the cast and crew grab their belongings and head to lounge area to wind down for a few minutes.

On closing night after the show ended, the entire cast and crew had made their way to the front of the building and I was alone in the dressing room finishing up. With my station finally clean, I started packing up my bag. Suddenly, the hair on the back of my neck started to stand up and a knot in my stomach began forming. I didn't know what was around, but I knew it was something that I needed to get away from. I quickly grabbed my bag, turned off all the lights and made my way to the door of the dressing room.

Barely through the entryway, I realized I was standing in the pitch dark and my intuition was screaming warnings to me. I began walking toward the ramp. Within two steps, I heard thunderous footsteps running toward me. The floor beneath my feet shook. Before I could move, I was surrounded by a thick, heavy presence. Praying it was Robert playing a joke on me, I screamed "Robert" and ran away from the area as fast as I could.

My husband Eric and Shawn were out near the entrance to the house when I came barreling out of the buffet area door. They looked at me like I had three heads before walking toward me.

"Are you okay?" Shawn said.

"What's wrong?" Eric said.

"Where's Robert?" I asked.

It had to have been him backstage messing with me.

"He's in the box office and has been for quite some time," Shawn replied.

"Who is backstage?" I demanded.

They all looked at each other then back to me.

"No one," they said.

It was that moment where terror set in. I realized that the entity that ran up on me was intentionally trying to frighten me. That being knew that I was alone and took complete advantage of my vulnerability.

I don't know what it was because of the dark. All I know is that the presence felt masculine, large and menacing. Maybe it is the same male energy from upstairs or maybe it was the shadow man. Maybe they are one in the same. I don't believe that I want to find out.

Another incident that has occurred near the ramp on multiple occasions is two taps on a person's shoulder. Melissa Dean experienced this during "Those Oldies but Goodies" in July 2016. Shawn experienced the same two taps in the same spot during "Lady Sings the Blues" in September 2016. While the taps are unwelcome, the impression given from the phantom fingers is somebody just wants to get by.

CHAPTER

9

Light Booth

The Harlequin light booth is located on the right side of the stage as you stand on it and has a window that looks out to the stage. Entering through a door from the tech area backstage, you step into a narrow room filled with more technical buttons than you could ever dream of.

At the far end of the small booth is a narrow ladder that leads up to a small square hole a.k.a. the entrance to the "grid." Translated for the non-tech folk like me, a grid is simply the area above the stage and house used to access stage lights, air conditioning units, room lighting, and anything else hidden by the ceiling panels.

The light booth is one of the creepiest rooms in the theater for two reasons: 1) it is a place that generally will offer up a paranormal experience or two, and 2) it is Robert's lair so he may be dancing any time you walk in there. This is not a good experience. Without humor, we would all die of boredom, so laugh people. Laugh.

Creature in the Hole

There are a few accounts in this book that made me walk away from my computer because reliving the event to talk about it can be as frightening as the experience itself. This experience is one of them.

In 2010, Robert and I were in the light booth and he was tasked with teaching me how to run the lights during a live production. He and I are dear friends and work extremely well together. Sometimes, we have far too much fun. Tonight was one of those nights. The show was going well and his directions were clear. We were both feeling confident and rather amused at ourselves.

Knowing the ghost stories around the theater, I asked him if he ever experienced anything in the light booth. He started to tell me a few things here and there.

Bang!

A noise came from above us in the grid.

We both looked up to the square opening. Nothing was there. Thinking it was just something that fell, we went back to our duties. Bang! We looked up, then at each other.

At this point, we weren't thinking it was anything paranormal. That was actually the furthest thing from our minds.

Because it was dark, I told him I was going to take a picture with my flip phone so that the flash would light up the area. Clearly, this was before flashlights existed on our phones, so I took out my phone and proceeded to take a flash picture.

Inside the light booth. The ladder leads to the square opening.
Photo Credit: Nikki Folsom

While the picture was being taken, I didn't see anything in the opening. I assumed nothing was wrong. It was when I looked at the photo on my camera, that my heart began to race.

The picture showed a creature staring back down at me from the small opening. It was hunkering down, but I estimated it to be about two to three feet tall standing up. The body of the creature was a pale, gray tone topped by a pointy head. The eyes were slanted, almost like a cat's eye. If I had to say it looked like something, I would describe it as a humungous grass hopper mixed with a small jester from medieval times.

With due haste, I peeled out of the light booth not even thinking about the fact that Robert couldn't leave. All I could hear were his soft screams.

"Nikki, come back," he said.

"Dammit, Nik, get back here," he pleaded.

"Oh my God," he began to panic.

"What was it?" aggravated at this point.

"Don't leave me in here alone," he demanded.

"Jesus Christ. I'm gonna kick your ass!" he yelled.

I gathered my wits about me and went back into the booth. Robert immediately started peppering me with questions. To avoid answering, I just showed him the picture.

His mouth dropped. He was stunned.

I know you are thinking show us the picture. Believe me, I would love to, but I can't find the flip phone that I took the picture on. I haven't given up that I will find it one day. That said, I had to tell the story because it is such an incredible account. To this day, I still cringe at the image of that creature in my head. To know it was looking down on us scares the hell out of me. How many times has he looked down on us since then?

Don't Be Afraid of the Dark

Gathering facts for this book required quite a bit of time. Time that I was happy to invest because it allowed me to spend time with people I simply adore. This particular time, it was Johnny.

It was a beautiful day and we agreed to meet for lunch at a local San Antonio grille. After sitting down and catching up on a million things, we changed the conversation to the information I was gathering on this book. In particular, we began talking about the shadow figure backstage. As Johnny began to share what he has seen on numerous occasions, chills ran down my spine.

"That's interesting on the shadow figure," he said.

"Why? Have you seen it too?" I asked.

He nodded, thought for a moment, then spoke.

"Yes. On the stage in the wings near the ramp."

My eyes grew wider as I listened to him. It's always great to receive validation on what you have seen. It makes me feel less crazy. Also, the more experiences I collected, the more the ramp is confirmed as a super active spot.

Johnny continued, "I've seen the shadow out of the corner of my eye" he said, then paused, "but that's not all I see."

"What do you mean?" I asked.

"There's what I would describe as a creature," he responded.

I'm pretty sure I jumped out of my seat as soon as the word "creature" left his mouth.

"Oh my God, Johnny!"

"What?"

"You saw it too? That's what *I* call it. 'The creature'!" I replied.

I began to share what Robert and I had experienced in the light booth. Johnny said that he could show me a picture of what it looks like. Stunned, I welcomed it. He explained that the image he was going to show me was from a Hollywood movie, but it was the closest thing to what he saw backstage.

Johnny went on his phone and googled the monster from the 2010 remake *Don't Be Afraid of the Dark*. As I had never seen that movie or even heard of it, I had no idea what the hell I would be looking at.

After finding the image, Johnny was hesitant to show me worried that I wouldn't sleep well. Finally, he handed me his phone.

My mouth dropped. I couldn't form a single word. This picture of a fictional Hollywood demon was almost identical to the creature that several of us have seen. Hell, it was almost identical to what I photographed. How is that even possible? What the hell are these things? Where do they come from? What do they want? All I can tell you is that it is still there and I do not want to run into it again.

Dedol's Touch

Every once in awhile, someone who has crossed over will stop in to say hi. Sometimes, it's at the strangest times and in the most unexpected ways. This is what happened to me.

In January 2006, I lost my Dedol. She was my maternal grandma and my everything. Losing her was simply devastating. I miss her every single day. Luckily, she sends me butterflies to remind me of her love and her presence.

In late 2011, Robert and I were in the light booth. He is always the first one in the booth, so he stands on the far right placing me to the left of him beside the door. We were working on a show while messing around with my new phone app "Ghost Radar." Intrigued by the colors of entities surrounding us, we started asking questions. When relevant words responded, we were almost giddy. Of course, our cautious skeptic sides came out and we decided that the matching words were a fluke. We laughed it off.

Distracted by the activities requiring our attention in the show, we stopped playing with the app. Suddenly, I felt someone touch my left arm from the door of the light booth.

Thinking it was Shawn needing help with a costume or being funny, I walked out the door to talk to him. Looking around, I didn't see anyone. Then, I could hear him singing on stage. In fact, the entire cast was on stage.

As strange as it was, I figured I was just imagining the touch. I looked down at my phone and the ghost app was still open. On my display, a word popped up - "touch." The wheels of my brain started to go super fast. I spoke to myself out loud.

"But how did it know?" I mumbled.

I almost passed out when the next word popped up - "Grandmother."

A sense of peace and love came over me. I placed my hand on

the part of my arm that was touched and softly rubbed it.

"Thank you, Dedol. I love you," I said.

I can't tell you if it was really my grandmother that touched me. All I can tell you is that it was extremely coincidental that the word "touch" came up within a minute of me being touched and the word "grandmother" came up. Whether or not it was her, love filled my whole spirit. I choose to believe it was her for no other reason than love never dies.

Scratched in the Light Booth

During the summer of 2010, the Harlequin hosted a another kids' summer camp that focused on honing dance, voice, and stage skills. The camp was a two week commitment with two weekends of great shows following the camp. Shawn was heavily involved in these productions because of his experience and talent. The children absolutely adored him. They still do.

Many times, I was acting as the stage manager for the shows while Shawn ran the lights from the booth. This particular show focused solely on Broadway and was crammed full of Broadway hits.

As the kids took the stage for one of the all-cast numbers, Shawn watched from the light booth. Suddenly, he felt an odd sensation on his arm. When he looked down, he saw a long scratch running down his arm. We still don't know what caused the scratch, but based on the activity, we have several suspects.

Voices

Like I've mentioned before, Robert says goodbye to Harlequin spirits every night. I believe he does it for two reasons: 1) to show them respect as individuals, and 2) to be sure the spirits don't follow us home. I believe it's a great practice and certainly helps maintain a good relationship with the good energies.

During my interview with Florence, she confirmed the she did the same thing for the same reasons, but she shared something else with me. Apparently, the spirits in the building know when we leave and our goodbye gives them notice that they are free to roam the building.

As Robert and I were building a set for the first show in 2017, I decided it was a good time to ask him a few questions about his experiences.

"When does it feel the scariest in the building to you?" I asked.

He thought for a second then spoke.

"Every so often after the lights are off, building is closed, doors are locked, and we are all walking to our cars, someone realizes that they forgot something. Then, I have to unlock the door, turn on the lights, and come back in the building. That is the most active time to me."

That seemed strange to me, but as he continued, it made sense.

"The theater is so quiet when you reenter the building. It's then when you are most likely to hear a disembodied voice, a distant whistle, a subtle scream, or something moving around in the house or on the stage," he said.

While he has heard numerous things in the super quiet theater, Robert told me about one occasion that stuck out in particular.

One night he was alone and had just finished locking up. He just reached his car when he remembered that he left his notebook in the light booth. Knowing that he had to go back in, he put his stuff in his car and headed back to the front doors of the building. He opened the doors and quickly moved through the lobby, then the house on his way to the light booth.

Robert stepped into the light booth and grabbed his notebook. As soon as his hand touched the book, he heard a woman's voice. She spoke extremely fast and sounded like she was talking through a walkie talkie or an old radio. The volume of her voice began softly but increased the longer he stayed in the building. The intensity increased as well.

He moved quickly to the door, said goodbye again, and left. After he got in his car, he realized in his frustration that he had forgotten to tell the spirits that he was coming back in.

Many people have heard this woman and these experiences have been reported all over the theater. Robert has heard her several times but mostly in the light booth.

Cigarette Smell

Similar to the rose perfume in the last chapter, another smell that has been lingering for many years is the smell of cigarettes. While this is something that many people experience all over the theater, the two most common places the scent is reported seem to be the light booth and the upstairs ladies room.

Robert recalled a recent experience with it in the light booth. One thing to note is that the smell never generates any sense of fear or anxiety, it just confuses the hell out of everyone.

Robert was running the lights for *The Birds* one night when an overwhelming smell of cigarettes permeated the booth. Thinking one of the cast members was standing at the back door smoking, he left the light booth to remind them of the smoking rules.

Seeing no one around, he quietly radioed Michael on the backstage headsets. Michael came running around to him from backstage.

"What?" Michael said.

"Are you smoking?" Robert asked.

"No, I quit weeks ago," Michael said.

"Do you smell that?" Robert said.

Michael started to sniff around in the air, then he smelled it too. We are still unable to attribute the smell to anything.

Because it's an old building with a rich history, the logical explanation could be the perfect mix in weather combined with the fabric or texture of an old item situated at the right place conjuring up odors from long ago. Then again, there could be another reason.

Looking through the archived information about the building, I discovered a court martial that occurred in 1950.

A corporal, who was a patron of the NCO Club at the time, was accused and found guilty of feloniously stealing property belonging to the US Army. What was the property you might wonder? Eleven cases of cigarettes.

Obviously, this could just be an odd coincidence. On the other hand, maybe a message is coming through from the other side. Either way, it is worth documenting for future encounters.

CHAPTER

IO

The Stairs

While the carpeted stairs that lead to the second floor look unassuming, even boring, there are countless stories associated with them. From the numerous reports of being pushed down them or being chased from upstairs, there is definitely something trying to get the attention of the living.

The stairs to the second floor.
Photo credit: Nikki Folsom

Florence shared a story with me about when she fell down the stairs. Many years ago, she was working during the day while two maintenance men were attending to some plumbing issues upstairs. After going upstairs to check on their progress, Florence was making her way back downstairs to the box office. She was just about to the bottom of the stairs, when she fell.

Before she knew what was happening, one of the maintenance men got to her and picked her up. She doesn't recall being pushed, so she has decided that she must have tripped. Either way, she always uses handrails now.

When Florence brought her psychic friends in to walk the building, both sensed the presence of a Native American man hovering around the staircase. While they shared that he spends most of his time at the bottom of the stairs, he would make his way up and down them as well. The male psychic even watched as the Native American touched the scarf that the female psychic wore.

The Native American man is not the only spirit seen near the stairs. A man, a little girl and boy, and what can only be called a "creature" have all been seen. Each experience has its own level of danger. Every time a person chooses to walk up or down these stairs, they take their personal safety into their own hands. Being pushed or chased down the stairs is frightening, but some of these stories in this chapter are beyond explanation.

Face in the Railing

The entry door to the box office is located directly at the bottom of the stairway to the second level. Because of its proximity to the upstairs rooms, we tend to work together across both floors. It's not uncommon to have someone upstairs looking for props or costumes yelling down to the person in the box office for their thoughts on it. It's quite convenient and helps us maintain extreme efficiency.

There are days that we don't need anything from upstairs, so we keep the lights off. It conserves energy, keeps the electric bill down, and most importantly, gives us a reason to avoid the upstairs.

Trying to think positively about the activity at the theater, we've started to approach every day like it will be quiet and uneventful. Unfortunately, those days are occurring less and less often.

Walking into a room or the theater itself, we can tell immediately upon entering what's in store. Sometimes, the day starts out fine and over time, the energy shifts while we are in the building. Unless you've experienced it, you will probably think we are crazy. The only way to describe it is that the air warns us. It feels like a thickness growing in the space, almost like a thunderstorm brewing. That's when the voices and sounds come from upstairs.

A few years ago, the Harlequin was showing a murder mystery. One particular night after the show, the cast members had changed, grabbed their stuff, and were heading out for the night.

The routine for "heading out" is to stop in to say goodbye to Robert in the box office because he's usually finishing the evening books.

That night, the cast members stopped in and Robert was congratulating them on a great show. As usual, they continue to chit chat for a few minutes. Suddenly, a loud noise came from darkness upstairs. Startled, Robert along with several of cast members moved to the bottom of the stairs to see what the noise was. Nothing but darkness.

Let me tell you, no one and I mean NO ONE goes upstairs in the dark, especially alone.

Thinking quickly, one cast member grabbed her cell phone and took a snapshot of the darkened stairway. The flash of the camera lit the stairs up briefly. To the relief of everyone standing there, nothing could be seen but the carpeted stairs.

A few of the cast members took a moment to review the picture. The stair rails that follow the stairs from the top of the staircase to the bottom seemed to be the main focal point.

At first glance, the photo revealed nothing. Laughing at their ability to be scared by the empty stairs and random noises, they showed Robert the picture. After looking at it for a minute, he spoke.

"Is that eyes?" Robert questioned.

The group laughed nervously and one of the cast members

grabbed the phone. He skeptically zoomed in on the photo. There, in the stair rail closest to the top of the stairs, was a face looking down at the camera. No body, no shadow - just a face. Gray in color with dark, sinister eyes and a gaping mouth, it was staring at the camera. After seeing the face, there was no mistaking it.

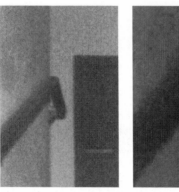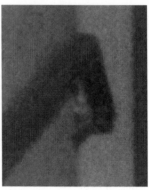

The railing at the Harlequin with the face. Photo on the right is a close up. Photo Credit: Jenn Harris

They passed the camera around and stood in disbelief at the photo. Frightened, the cast members exited quickly leaving Robert alone in the building.

I have reviewed the picture myself. As your resident buzzkill, I wondered if the face could be pareidolia - a phenomenon that occurs when your mind creates something from a pattern that isn't actually there. Of course, I'd be the first to dismiss it. Unfortunately, I've seen that face before. It's the face of the creature.

Violet's Invisible Friend

Violet is one of the most energetic and fun loving young ladies that you will ever meet. At five years old, she owns the Harlequin as soon as she walks through the door.

Sassy, sweet, and absolutely adorable, she could sell ice cream to a snowman and entertain the meanest scrooge. Violet is Katie Molina's niece and I swear, she is the epitome if "Mini Me" when it comes to Katie. I adore them both.

Violet comes to see every show that Katie is in at least once every run. As expected, she was there for the Christmas show in 2016.

After the show ended, Marcus, Katie's brother and Violet's uncle, was chasing her around the theater as she sprinkled her magic everywhere she went.

He began to notice that she was kept running back and looking up the dark stairs.

"I want to go see the little girl," Violet said.

Knowing that no one was upstairs and Violet was the only child at the theater that night, Marcus blew it off. Violet didn't let up.

"She wants me to come upstairs and play with her."

Pretending not to hear that comment, Marcus brought her back to the lounge and tried to distract her. Suddenly, she darted to the bottom of the dark stairs. He ran after her, fearing she might get hurt. When he got to her, she was standing at the bottom of the stairs waving up to the darkness at the top.

"Who are you waving to, Violet?" Marcus asked.

"My friend."

"What friend?"

"The little girl."

"It's dark up there, Violet. There's no one is up there."

"Yes, she is. She's waving at me and wants me to come up and play with her," Violet said.

Marcus picked her up and carried her back to the lounge.

While I'm confident Violet saw the little girl ghost that night, I know Marcus had no desire to see her. And he sure didn't want Violet venturing up there.

Disappearing Feet

Every once in awhile, Florence would need a day off. On those days, Bruce would come in, cover the box office and take care of any other odd jobs that needed attention.

Because he spent a great deal of time at the theater, he wasn't bothered by being alone. Between working the box office and cleaning up here and there, he was able to keep himself busy by focusing on critical items.

After finishing some work in the house, he was coming back

to the box office to finish up paperwork. He had no more than sat down at the desk when he heard a loud noise come from upstairs. Knowing he was the only one in the theater, he walked to the bottom of the stairs to see if he could hear anything.

As he got to the bottom of the stairs and looked up, he saw the cuff of a man's pant leg passing by the top of the stairs toward the men's room. Thinking someone broken in, he ran up the stairs yelling at the intruder. He reached the top of the stairs and turned the lights on, fully illuminating the hallway. Slowly, he went room by room until he had investigated the entire upstairs.

No one was there.

Three Finger Push

As I descended the stairs with Florence during our walk through, she held tightly to the stair rail stopping midway down to share an experience she remembered from years ago with an old performer, Don Carpenter. Don, an extremely talented actor who once graced the Harlequin stage, wasn't afraid of anything especially when it came to ghosts. Yes, he heard the stories and encountered a few questionable things, but that wasn't enough to frighten him. An absolute "cautious skeptic," Don was a person that had to be hit over the head with it to believe it.

One afternoon, he was upstairs talking to Florence in the office. They wrapped up everything that needed to be cared for and decided to head downstairs. Florence started down the stairs first and continued the conversation with Don who was a few steps behind her.

She reached the bottom and turned back to Don to continue their discussion. As he reached the third step from the bottom, a look of confusion came across his face. Suddenly, he fell down the remaining stairs.

Running to help him, Florence made sure that he wasn't hurt and proceeded to help him up.

"What happened?" she asked.

"You aren't going to believe it," he responded.

"You can't tell me anything I haven't heard before," she challenged.

Don explained that when he reached the third step from the bottom, he felt three fingers aggressively jab themselves into the middle of his back, pushing him down the stairs. He was in disbelief as he fell all the way to the bottom.

> *There have been numerous reports of being pushed down the stairs from people of all ages. I have one of a young girl, approximately ten years of age who was pushed from the fifth stair from the bottom three separate times. I also have reports of being pushed from the top of the stairs. We don't know who the pusher is, but someday we hope to find out.*

CHAPTER

II

Upstairs

The second floor of the Harlequin consists of two costume rooms, a prop room, a musical instrument room, an office, a rehearsal hall, a ladies lounge, a men's room and two miscellaneous rooms. Most of the decor is from years gone by with a splash of costumes, props, and other items sprinkled around.

Back in the days of the NCO Club, the upstairs housed two bars, the ladies lounge, the men's room and quite a few storage rooms. The layout was almost identical with the exception of the top left of the stairs. It was once one large bar instead of a costume and prop room.

At the theater today, the upstairs is used mostly for rehearsals and storage. When in use, you can usually find several people upstairs. If the lights are off, only a handful of people are willing to go up there. Some consider this space the most terrifying area of the building. If we have to go up alone, it is for a damn good reason.

On a few occasions, I have felt quite brave and started up the stairs alone. I would reach the top of the stairs, feel nothing, and go about my business like the cowardly lion who just got his courage. Other times, I haven't even gotten to the top of the stairs before my "spider senses" start going nuts forcing me back downstairs.

I remember one afternoon, I was alone and headed upstairs on a mission. Convinced that if I went up, got what I need, and came right back down, everything would be fine. Not so.

As I reached the middle of the hall upstairs, I walked into an invisible wall of energy accompanied by a strong musty smell literally stopping me in my tracks. It felt like an extremely thick layer of air. In my mind, I could almost hear someone saying "go back downstairs NOW!"

When something takes the time and energy to conjure up a feeling that strong, you listen. I turned around right where I stood and fled back down stairs. I'm sure that I looked like a twelve year old running out of a fun-house, but I didn't care.

I was completely out of breath when I got to the lounge where Suzy watched as I tried to gather myself. After explaining what had just happened, she agreed to go back up with me.

Together, we walked up the stairs to the same spot I had just run from. Nothing was there. No thick air. No musty smell. Nothing. I grabbed the costumes I went up for and we went back downstairs.

While this experience with two of us turned out well, going upstairs in pairs isn't always comfortable. I cannot tell you the number of times Shawn and I or Robert and I have gone up together and still felt incredibly uneasy.

Another common occurrence upstairs involves the lights. They turn on and off by themselves especially in the upstairs ladies lounge, men's room and the rehearsal room.

Before we leave the theater every night, we do a sweep of the building to ensure that all the lights are off. I can assure you that every single night the building is dark when we walk out, lock the door, walk away, and leave the premises.

On numerous occasions, we will drive away from the theater only to find the lights still on in one of those rooms. At first, the people closing would park their car, return to the building, unlock the door, and make their way to the room with the lights on and turn them off. It wouldn't matter.

As soon as they drove away, the lights would be back on. We have learned to just leave them on. If the spirits want them on, they are staying that way whether we like it or not.

Man in the Hallway

One of the things that I find rewarding is organizing. This works to the benefit of my family and the Harlequin. Several years ago, I took on the task of organizing the small wardrobe room. In this instance, I was upstairs alone. For some reason, I didn't feel afraid, threatened or even bothered. It could be because the task started about three o'clock in the afternoon and the sun was shining brightly outside.

Downstairs, the cast was rehearsing feverishly for an upcoming show. I was happy knowing that I would be able to work uninterrupted for hours. Rummaging through the costumes, shoes, and props around the room, I lost track of time. When I finally looked up, it was dark outside.

As I was wrapping things up in the room, I heard movement in the hallway. Thinking it was one of the cast members coming up to check on me, I called out.

"I'm fine."

No response.

Knowing these people, no response is not an option. They are performers, so they talk to everyone. I moved to the door and peeked my head out. A man was walking down the hallway and turned to make his way down the stairs. He was in my line of vision for no more than twenty seconds.

"Hey!" I called out.

He just kept walking. At the time, I didn't think anything of it. I didn't know who he was, but I shrugged, assuming that he was there for a reason. Maybe, he was a maintenance man checking something.

I wrapped everything up and made my way downstairs into the house where the cast was still rehearsing. I took a quick look around the room and noticed the man from upstairs wasn't there. I even made sure to look to see if anyone in the cast was wearing the same clothes. Nope.

"Hey, where did that guy go?" I asked.

"What guy?" Shawn said.

"The guy that was just upstairs. He was in a blue jump suit."

The entire cast looked at each other then back at me. About three of them started to question me about what he looked like. I explained exactly what I saw. A Caucasian man about six feet tall with sandy blonde hair wearing what looked like a one piece navy flight suit. My grandfather was a carpenter and I remember watching him go off to work in a very similar zip up suit.

"What did he say?" someone asked.

"Nothing."

"Nothing?"

Again, they looked at each other. Then, they all started talking at once.

"Oh my God, you saw a ghost!"

"It's the mean man!"

"No, I didn't see a ghost. It couldn't have been," I said.

It couldn't have been a ghost. The man was as solid as you and me. There was no transparency whatsoever. Ghosts aren't solid, right? I took another look at everyone in the room and realized not a single person even remotely resembled the man I had seen.

"Wait a minute. You mean to tell me someone just came in and walked upstairs without any of y'all seeing him?"

"That's not possible," the director said.

"Why not?" I responded.

"The doors are locked, so the only people in the building are in this room," replied the director.

That's when the fear kicked in for me. It wasn't during the experience; it was well after when I was reflecting on it.

After I began talking about the man, other individuals associated with the theater started to talk about their glimpses of this spirit.

I can't explain why I didn't sense his presence or why he didn't take advantage of my vulnerability. Supposedly, he is one of the meaner energies at the theater and there I was - a woman alone upstairs isolated away from the rest of the people in the building. Had I screamed, I'm not sure anyone would have heard me.

Now, thinking about how truly defenseless I had been, I am

gobsmacked at how stupid I was to have allowed myself to be that vulnerable. I assure you I will not put myself in that position again.

Spiritual Showdown

As I write this account, I realize how much time I spend tidying up the costume rooms at the theater. It seems that is where this next experience occurred as well. C'est la vie. Here I am back in the small costume room working on the organization of the room. Again. This time, I had Samantha Eberle, Ashton's bestie and a Harlequin performer herself, upstairs with me.

Samantha has spent many years at the theater, so she has heard all the stories. Luckily for her, she had never had a full-on experience, but she was very curious to hear the accounts of people who had.

An app I had on my phone at the time was an EMF (Electro Magnetic Frequency) detector. I used it sometimes to see if it would give me an EMF reading. Its success rate was hit or miss, so I didn't give it much credence.

To keep Samantha occupied while I worked, I sent her to the ladies lounge directly across the hall with the EMF app open. Every once in a while, she would yell over to me and ask me questions to which I would respond with my best guess.

"How do you know its here?" she asked.

"The airs changes."

"What do you mean the air changes?"

"I don't know how to describe it."

"What does it feel like?"

"Um. I guess it feels like the room gets really humid - like a super hot day. But the air isn't moist just thick."

"Oh….."

Her tone had changed and I could tell that she was starting to get nervous. Before I could say anything, the app on my phone started to make a loud screaming noise that I had never heard before. I had barely opened my mouth to talk to Samantha when she burst into the room.

Confused, I took the phone and looked at it. The EMF needle was pinned on the opposite side of the dial indicating that the meter was maxed out. Samantha's eyes were like saucers.

"What does that mean?" she asked.

I wasn't sure what to say. The app had never done that before and I had no explanation. Suddenly, the room was filled with a heavy thickness and we found ourselves surrounded by a threatening, masculine energy. I was terrified. Knowing that Samantha would be taking her clue from me on how to react, I tried to remain as calm and collected as possible.

Just as I was pulling her close to me, I could feel another energy enter the room - an extremely protective energy. It felt like a mother bear charging in to protect her cubs.

I don't know why I didn't just run, but I stood there with my arm around Samantha feeling the showdown between the energies. Not sure how but I knew we were supposed to wait.

Suddenly, I felt the feminine energy take over. It's as though she stepped in and said, "You can move safely downstairs now." I took advantage of her kindness quickly moving Samantha and myself out of there. I still can't explain the experience, but I thank God every day that good won over evil that evening.

Chased

Recently, Shawn and I were upstairs looking at costumes for an upcoming show. Costume shopping upstairs is a fairly common event for us. Well, shopping in general is a common event for us, but that is another story. We spent a good fifteen to twenty minutes in the small wardrobe room and music room going through various things.

Feeling confident that we had reviewed all of our options upstairs, we turned the lights off in the smaller rooms and made our way down the hallway. We stopped by the light switch for the overall hallway in front of the rehearsal room, briefly to confirm we had and what we needed.

Satisfied with our finds, Shawn turned off the hallway lights. We were immediately enveloped in pitch black darkness. That's when the footsteps started from the music room at the far end of the hall. Moving quickly toward us, they grew increasingly louder and stronger.

Shawn and I made a beeline for the stairs. Instinct told me to turn my phone flashlight on and shine it behind us as we raced down the stairs. As soon as the flashlight illuminated the top of the stairs, the footsteps stopped.

I have no idea what possessed me to shine my flashlight, but it worked. Maybe the magic flashlight that we used as little kids use to scare away monsters isn't so far-fetched after all.

CHAPTER

12

Rehearsal Room

As you enter through the double doors to the right of the stairs, you find yourself in the rehearsal room. This large, carpeted space is filled with furniture, wall art, mirrors, costumes, and a whole host of things used in the theater and on the sets. The room itself is square with a smaller square in the far corner that wraps around slightly.

Used for play rehearsals, auditions, choreography practice, photo shoots, and anything else we need, this area could really be described as our jack of all trades area.

As we understand it, this room was once a bar when the NCO club was active in the sixties. This is the room that the mean man was rumored to have been killed in.

With a bar in its past, I'm sure this room has seen its share of laughter and tears. This alone could explain the host of paranormal experiences in this room such as doors opening and closing, disembodied voices, apparitions in the mirrors, and people being bruised.

Years ago, there was a television in the rehearsal room. It was discovered by accident that if you leave it on with old cowboy movies playing, the activity in the room will decrease. If by chance someone turned the television off, the activity would pick up until it was on again. Unfortunately, cable was deemed unnecessary, so the television is no longer in the room.

To the right of the rehearsal room, there is a small walk-in closet. When the building was the NCO, this room was used as the pantry for the main upstairs bar. Today, it is used mainly for storage.

One day years ago, Florence was taking her friends on a tour of the theater. They stopped briefly in this small room to talk about its history. Out of nowhere, they could hear the faint sounds of a woman or child sobbing. As they listened, the volumes of the cries increased. Then within an instant, the sound was gone.

While I've related many paranormal experiences in this book, there are even more accounts of strange things that have happened. Florence's memory of the sobbing is only one. There's just not enough pages to recount them all.

Opening Doors

One of the most common happenings reported in this room is the opening and closing of the doors. I personally have witnessed it on numerous occasions over the years. One of my experiences occurred during a live show. The director left the power cord to her laptop in the rehearsal room. As the show was starting, she realized that her computer battery was going to die. She grabbed me and asked me to run up to the room to get the cord.

While I was apprehensive, I knew there was no one else who could run the errand, so off I went praying that the lights were on in the hall upstairs. Reaching the bottom of the stairs and seeing the lights on, I thanked God the entire way up. After scanning the room and grabbing the cord, I was thrilled that I was able to get upstairs and get what I needed uneventfully.

I thought too quick.

As I exited the room, I closed the double doors behind me. Relived, I was about three steps from the stairs when the doors suddenly swung open. Terrified, I wasn't going to hang around to see what was going to come out of the room.

Downstairs, I handed the director the cord, and told her under no uncertain terms that I would not be doing that ever again. She laughed and had me tell her what happened.

Another night, my friend, Steve and his wife came to see one of our musicals. While he has heard the stories of the theater, he is a perfect example of "cautious skeptic" thinking everything has a logical explanation.

After the show, I was telling him about some of our recent experiences. He listened, laughing at the fact that I actually believed I saw or heard some of this stuff. My husband Eric, another skeptic, was close by. He asked Steve if he would like to go upstairs to see the rooms. He eagerly agreed.

Because I had to finish up my work downstairs, Eric and Steve headed upstairs alone. In my mind, they were two grown men. They would be fine.

Not five minutes had passed before they were back downstairs. I have given tours upstairs before. They are never that quick especially with people as curious as these two guys. As I looked at there faces, I knew something had happened.

Was it rude to laugh or even say I told you so? I didn't say anything but I assure you, I thought it as they walked over to me.

"What's wrong?" I asked.

"You are not going to believe this," Steve said.

"Try me," I said.

Eric proceeded to share this experience because Steve was so freaked out he could barely speak.

They had just gotten to the top of the stairs where Eric was telling Steve about some of the happenings that have been reported from the men's room and the rehearsal room. They continued walking down toward the ladies lounge.

As the passed the rehearsal room, they noticed the doors were shut. Both of them had just reached the middle of the hallway when the doors to the rehearsal room opened, powered by an unseen entity because no other humans were up there. Neither Steve nor Eric went any farther. They made a beeline for the stairs.

I couldn't hold it in anymore.

"I told you so," I said.

I didn't ask any more questions because I was giggling non-stop. All I could picture was two six foot tall professional men running from an invisible energy who opened a set of doors. I shouldn't have laughed because I know how frightening that is. But the picture in my head of them running like little kids was nothing short of hilarious.

Another door opening experience didn't scare any of us. It was simply confirmation that something was present and wanted to join us.

A few years ago, we were rehearsing for a production of *A Few Good Men*. Because we can work uninterrupted upstairs, the cast chose to rehearse in the rehearsal room. By force of habit, we closed the doors behind us after we went in.

We began rehearsing act one and were engrossed in the play for about thirty minutes when we heard someone trying to open the doors. Thinking it was our imaginations, we ignored it. Finally, after several minutes of the doors rattling, Robert was exasperated.

"You can come in now," he said.

As soon as he said it, the doors opened on their own as though someone was walking in. No one was there. The entire cast was stunned.

Bruises

One thing I can tell you about myself is that I bruise easily - always have. Because of this, I tend to dismiss bruises that I find on my body. This was different. I wasn't the only one with the bruises this time.

In 2010, I was tasked with pulling potential costumes for the upcoming show while the cast was rehearsing downstairs. Because the costumes were in the rehearsal room, I didn't feel like lugging them all downstairs just then.

It was early in the afternoon and the whole cast had just been upstairs with me, so I felt completely comfortable remaining in the room. After about an hour, I was pleased with the selection of the costumes and walked downstairs to the lounge.

Several of the performers were sitting at the table and I sat down with them. We were talking for a few minutes when one of the guys looked at me funny.

"What is on your arm?" he said.

I started to look along with the others sitting around me.

"Where?" I asked.

He pointed to my right bicep. I gasped when I saw it. It was four bruises lined up as though someone had gripped my arm so tightly that it caused bruising.

"Did someone grab you?" another cast member asked.

I was sure that nothing occurred that would bruise me like that. And I was even more sure that I did not have those marks when I got to the theater. While the bruising pattern was strange, I assumed that I did something stupid somewhere along the line and just didn't realize it.

The next morning, I was getting ready to go to the theater and Ashton decided that she was going with me. We were both in great moods and excited to see the dress rehearsal of the show.

Knowing that I had the task of bringing the costumes downstairs, I asked Ashton if she wanted to help. At that time, Ash was ten and not all that excited about hauling costumes down the stairs. That was fine with me. She was going to keep me company while I went up and down the stairs.

We got to the theater and got set up to transfer the items one by one. Ash was sitting in the rehearsal room as I went up and down the stairs. While she has never been comfortable upstairs alone, she was playing her music and knew I would only be gone for about thirty seconds at a time.

After one of my trips downstairs, I was distracted by questions from the cast about their costumes. I'll admit it. I'm easily distracted especially with sparkly dresses.

I had been downstairs for several minutes when Ashton came barreling into the lounge. The look of fear on her face made me feel immediate guilt. She looked terrified. Why the hell did I leave her alone up there?

I hugged her and told her everything was okay. She loved watching the girls try on their dresses, so she quickly forgot about her fear. Relieved, I went back to bring down the remaining dresses.

When my work was completed, I sat down beside Ashton at the table. My eyes were drawn to her right bicep. I almost passed out when I saw them. Bruises in the shape of fingerprints. Four of them identical to the ones on my arm.

Now, I know that my bruises were not obtained through careless actions on my part. They were deliberately placed there by some invisible force lurking upstairs. The anger in me boiled over. How could that entity mess with my baby? Me? Fine. Her? No way. I was livid. Livid but smart. I had no idea what was up there, so I knew better than to provoke it.

At this time, no one else in the theater has been bruised in such a way. I'm not saying it didn't happen. I just don't know any more about it if it has.

Person in the Picture

Every once in a while, someone will get brave enough to do a ghost hunt in the building. Amateur and professional, these are always fun and interesting.

Luckily, I was able to tag along with Brad and Barry one night during one. While it was extremely interesting and I'm extremely appreciative of the experience, I can't help but walk away frustrated because the spirits weren't displaying the same behaviors we see when no one else is around. It's terribly disappointing.

During another ghost hunt, Shawn's sister, Brittany was going through the rooms upstairs. She happened to snap a picture of a person behind the chair. Robert pointed out that it was a man. I thought it was a little girl based on size. Of course, it could be the paredolia effect too. What do you see?

Some see nothing in this photo while others have seen a man crouching down and a little girl. Photo Credits: Brittany Kjos

CHAPTER
13
Ladies Lounge

The upstairs ladies lounge is a versatile and unique restroom at the far right end of the hallway. Entering the space, you follow a U shaped turn into the lounging area. Florence confirmed that this was used as a dressing room for cast members years ago.

After passing the large lighted mirror area, you can walk through an open doorway into four stalls and two sinks. This room could easily hold ten or more ladies dressing for a show.

I've seen this area take on more themes than I can count - a dressing room from the twenties, a lounge from the seventies, a rave from the eighties, and an explosion of sequin dresses from multiple eras. It has even housed a massive wall of costume boxes. The decor depends on the set design at the moment and what is available to decorate with.

About a fifth of the size of the rehearsal room, many musical rehearsals take place here as well. It is a more intimate space with stronger acoustics making it much easier for the cast to hear musical parts when rehearsing. In addition, the restroom section is perfect for warming up and singing through solos.

With reports of doors opening on their own, an apparition of a lady in a green dress, and balls of light disappearing through the entryway, the ladies' lounge has had its share of reported paranormal events. Additionally, this room tends to be the place that many people are hesitant to enter alone because this is one of the places where the shift in the air is most prevalent.

Entity in the Bathroom

Ironically, Shawn's most frightening experience occurred in the ladies lounge. During a rehearsal in 2010, the full cast was singing through songs in the rehearsal room. They reached a part in the rehearsal that required only the girls, so Shawn took the opportunity to use the ladies lounge to sing through a few of his solos.

Typically, the performers will use their cell phones to play music, then sing along to the tune. This time, Shawn was in the ladies lounge sitting on the sink facing the bathroom stalls. He was mid-note when something forcefully kicked open the door in the stall directly in front of him. The door stopped dead in mid-swing, like something had caught it and was holding it open.

Instantly, his voice went silent and the air was taken right out of Shawn's mouth. In shock, he couldn't breathe. He couldn't even move. After what felt like an hour, whatever it was released its grip and Shawn ran full speed to the rehearsal room where the other performers were.

Knowing something was wrong by the look on his face, they rallied around him trying to calm him down. He took a few moments, gathered his thoughts, then shared the experience with the cast.

To this day, every time Shawn enters the ladies lounge to warm up, he tells the ghosts that he is going to sing and asks them nicely to leave him alone. So far, they have adhered to his request.

Lady in the Green Dress

Over the years, the Harlequin has seen its share of volunteers come through its doors. Many of these individuals were retired ladies and gentlemen who loved the theater and were looking for a way to contribute. Because of their age, many have passed but the appreciation for their contribution to the Harlequin lives on.

One such volunteer was Minnie, a regular usher at the theater who loved spending time in the building. Minnie was beloved by employees, performers, and fellow volunteers because of her sassy attitude and funny stories.

When she passed, the employees of the theater had a portrait painted of her and proceeded to hang it in her honor. (A picture of the portrait is on page 27.) Years have passed since then and the portrait has been moved around hundreds of times. It's even been a part of show sets. Currently, the painting is propped against the wall in the rehearsal room.

Sometimes, people who love a particular location choose to remain there and we have often wondered if Minnie roams the halls of the Harlequin. In 2009, we got our answer.

During the years of the Harlequin's children's program, there could've been anywhere from twenty to forty kids taking classes or rehearsing throughout the week. Because of the main stage shows occurring downstairs, the youngsters sometimes rehearsed upstairs. They were often split up into groups spread across different rooms to work on their group songs.

After wrapping rehearsal one evening, all the kids slowly made their way downstairs chattering and laughing. One of the youngest and bubbliest was Jordyn who was six at the time. Following the group downstairs, she was uncharacteristically quiet and walked over to her teachers.

"I don't want to rehearse upstairs any more," she said.

Because of her age and level of adorable, everyone was overly protective of her. When she had an issue, she immediately got a concerned reaction.

"Why?" they asked.

"The lady in the green dress scares me," Jordyn answered.

Jordyn was so young that she didn't know about stories associated with the theater. She certainly didn't know about Minnie.

At that time, her portrait was being stored not displayed. The teachers though did know about Minnie and it took them about three seconds to put two and two together.

Realizing they they were talking to a child and trying to prevent any unnecessary fear, the teachers did not talk about what they knew. They calmly asked Jordyn about what she saw.

"What lady in the green dress?" they asked.

Jordyn explained that she and her group were working on their song in the hallway when she saw something moving out of the corner of her eye at the far end of the hall. When she looked to see what it was, there was a woman in a green dress staring at her angrily. After a few seconds, the lady disappeared into the ladies lounge.

The teachers told her not to worry about the lady and attempted to calm her fears. After many hugs and a few pieces of candy, Jordyn forgot all about it and went home with her parents. It wasn't until a few weeks later that Jordyn received her validation.

Someone had been rummaging through the rehearsal room

looking for props and set pieces. In their frenzy, they left the room a bit disorganized with random art work all over the room. When the kids arrived for rehearsal, they had to work around the rearranged rehearsal room. As they picked their sitting spot, Jordyn noticed Minnie's portrait. She got up, walked over to it, and pointed.

"That's her," she said.

"Who?" the teacher responded.

"The lady in the green dress that I saw walking into the ladies room," she said.

Luckily, there was not a main stage show this night because the teacher gathered up the kids and moved them to the lounge for the rehearsal.

Phantom Legs

When I was talking with Florence, she shared an interesting account that she received from a patron long ago. One night, a woman had come to see one of the productions with a group of her friends. The show had started, the cast was backstage, and the audience was in their seats enjoying act one.

Florence was in the box office working on her paperwork and had just stepped out to check on how the show was going. A woman came out of the theater to go upstairs to use the ladies room. Smiling at Florence, she made her way upstairs.

Within a few minutes, she was back downstairs looking white as a ghost. Pardon the pun.

"Are you okay?" Florence asked.

The woman was beside herself as she related her experience to Florence.

She had gone upstairs to the ladies lounge. When she arrived, the lights in the lounge were on; however, the lights in the actual restroom section were off. It wasn't a problem because she knew where the light switch was.

As she approached the the stall area, she noticed a pair of legs under one of the stall doors. Thinking that a woman was in the restroom and the lights had gone out on her, she flipped the switch and the lights came on. When she didn't get a reaction from the lights coming on, she looked back down toward the legs in the stall. They were gone.

The woman didn't even take the time to use the restroom. She immediately came downstairs to find someone to accompany her back to the room.

Large Orb

Walking through the Harlequin, you never know what you will see or when you will see it. Weeks can go by and nothing strange occurs (or at least it isn't noticed), then BAM, the next day all hell breaks loose. Between the living and the dead, there's never a dull moment.

One afternoon, Johnny was working with a cast of folks preparing for an upcoming show. When we are in our preparation groove, we work heads down. Spirits or not, the show must go on. On this day, the costumes were being finalized for dress rehearsal and Johnny remembered one of the pieces was still in the ladies lounge.

After making his way up the stairs, he turned right to walk down the hall. As he lifted his head, he saw a small ball of light hovering in front of the ladies lounge. The ball itself reminded him of an opal with incredible colors veined in a thick white mist. A feminine energy surrounded him leaving him with a soft and welcoming feeling. Mystified, he watched as it grew until it was touching the floor and ceiling emitting a beautiful bright light. Eventually, the ball disappeared into the ladies lounge taking the bright light with it.

Johnny is still not sure who or what the entity was, but he is sure that is was sent from a loving and peaceful place.

CHAPTER

14

The Grid

The grid is the space located above the house and stage. This room holds air conditioning units, light riggings, extra materials, and access to wiring throughout the building.

There are two entrances to this room. From downstairs, the grid is accessed through the a square entryway via a ladder in the light booth. The main entryway is though the double doors in the upstairs hallway.

I hate these doors. They have a mind of their own, opening and closing when they want to, not necessarily when a human opens them. Typically, the only people that venture into that area are Robert and the HVAC people.

In the early days of the Harlequin, this room housed two huge dimmer lights attached to the house and a large projection room, which is now a closet. Back in the day, Florence had to go upstairs with her portable headset, listen for the cue to lower the house lights, then execute the dimming procedure.

Thank God, this process has been improved. Now, we operate the lights from downstairs. The strange thing is that even though the controls for the lights are downstairs, the lights in the grid will turn on mid-show when everyone in the building is downstairs. Curious, very curious.

Creature in the Grid

Florence and I had a fabulous time walking through the building swapping stories. But when I brought up the some of the experiences in the grid, her face went into deep thought and her eyes lit up with surprise.

"Oh my. I completely forgot about that," she said.

"About what?" I asked.

"The creature," she responded.

That was two times now. First Johnny, now Florence. Both had referred to this thing as "the creature." I almost fell over because she told me this story after I had already documented mine about this same entity. Then, she remembered that Bruce often referred to something that he saw as "the imp." While she couldn't recall experiences that Bruce has had with this imp, she did say that he talked of it often. We took a moment to discuss the craziness of the happenstance, then I asked her to share with me what she knew about it.

It was many years ago that Jason, a Military Policeman, volunteered his time and energy at the Harlequin. The theater felt extremely lucky to have him. Intelligent, protective, focused, and logical, he was used to dealing with and able to filter through any dramatic nonsense. He was and always will be considered a friend of the theater.

Because he was mainly focused on the technical aspects of the theater, quite a bit of his time was spent in the grid, light booth, and backstage.

One evening, Jason was alone working in the grid readying the lights for an upcoming show. Focused on his mission, he tuned out everything and everyone. After completing an exceptionally complicated wiring reroute, he decided to lay his head back and rest for a moment.

His head had barely touched its resting spot when he heard a strange noise coming from across the room. Jason looked around, puzzled, trying to identify the source of the noise. Seeing nothing, he leaned back to rest head again.

Before he could even put his head down, he heard the noise again. His head shot up in the direction of the disturbance and he caught a glimpse of something moving.

Knowing something was there and thinking it was an animal, Jason slowly scanned the area. There, in the shadows, he saw it! A strange looking creature with an odd shaped head and large dark eyes sat crouched down in the shadows looking back at him.

Feeling the thickness grow in the air, the hair on Jason's arms stood up and his stomach turned in knots. He was confused trying to determine what this thing was. Suddenly, it rose.

Slightly hunched over at no more than than three feet high, Jason could hear it growling from across the room. Desperate to get out of there, he dropped everything and crawled as fast as his legs would carry him.

Part of the Grid.
Photo Credit: Nikki Folsom

Jason got off the grid, ran out the doors, down the hall, and flew down the stairs. When questioned about what he was running from, all he could say was a demonic creature. Jason was adamant. It wasn't a person and there is no animal that looks like that.

The Growl

Because Robert has had so many experiences in the building, I was curious to find out what his "most frightening" moment has been. As he began sharing it with me, he shuttered.

During a tech week for a musical a few years ago, one of the lights went out over the stage and he needed to go to the grid to replace it.

Getting to the top of the stairs, Robert noticed that the air felt strange. Considering how thick and menacing it felt, he considered going back downstairs but remembered the light that had gone out. Knowing he had no choice, he ventured into the grid to change it out. He had just started to make his way across the grid when his senses took over and his body froze. Something was there. Close but not visible, he felt its presence near him.

Suddenly, he heard a loud, threatening growl. He decided that the light was going to wait and abandoned his mission to change it out that night.

Robert has heard this growl in the light booth multiple times. We have no idea what the source of the growl is, but based on the level of threat it emanates, it doesn't feel like a good entity.

CHAPTER
15
Men's Room

The upstairs men's room is located at the top of the stairs and to the left. I can probably count on one hand the number of times that I've actually seen someone use this room.

Smaller than the spacious ladies lounge, this restroom has three stalls, a urinal and two sinks. There is absolutely no decor, and boring is the kindest description I can offer. Space is limited in here because men just don't need as much room as women when doing their business. My best guess would be that the room could hold approximately five men at a time.

While the list of activities reported in this room is short, the experiences are unnerving - disembodied voices and physical contact. This short list doesn't mean other incidents haven't occurred, it just means these are the ones that were shared with me.

Threatening Voice

People who work or volunteer at the theater try to use the restrooms upstairs during shows to keep the downstairs restrooms available to the public. Most people go upstairs, do their business quickly, and came back downstairs to continue their tasks. Eric, on the other hand, would disappear into this bathroom just to avoid the crowds.

During one particular sold-out show, Eric told me that he was going upstairs to spend some quality alone time. This was his way of telling me that he was going to get away from the crowd and read the news. Whether he was disappearing to do his business or not, I didn't care. I just wanted him to be comfortable.

As I have stated before, Eric is incredibly skeptical, so his viewpoint on experiences at the theater is extremely valuable.

I can't recall how long he was gone, but it couldn't have been more than than fifteen minutes because it occurred during an intermission. When I looked up, he was staring at me dumbfounded. I couldn't tell if he was frightened or confused. One thing I was certain of was that he was in disbelief.

"What's wrong?" I asked.

"You aren't going to believe this but…" he said.

If I had a dollar for every time someone said to me, "You aren't going to believe this - but," I'd be a billionaire.

Anyway, he continued explaining what occurred in exact detail. As he ascended the stairs, he debated about sitting in the hallway since he really didn't need to use the restroom. He just wanted to browse through the news. At the last minute, he decided to sit in a stall just to have some privacy in case someone else came upstairs.

Sitting quietly minding his own business, he heard a woman's voice faintly. He stopped, looked up, and listened for a moment, then dismissed it as probably a woman talking downstairs.

Within a minute, a loud, clear female voice sternly and threateningly said, "GET OUT!" from directly beside him.

Knowing he was alone in the room and absolutely alone in the stall, he bolted out of the men's room, down the stairs, and made a beeline for me.

After telling me about his experience, he didn't talk about it again for several days. It wasn't until we got to the theater the following week that Eric realized the validity of his story.

One of Eric's favorite people to talk to was Gerry, the bartender who use to work in the lounge. They got along well and loved sharing stories. He talked to her for hours enjoying every minute of it. About a week after Eric's experience, we were at the theater. Gerry was setting up the bar while Eric and I kept her company.

"Did you tell Gerry what happened to you?" I asked.

He shot me a quick "don't talk about it look."

"No he didn't," Gerry said.

Reluctantly, Eric began to retell his previous week's experience to Gerry. As he spoke, her face lost all color and she stopped working on the bar set-up. He finished the story and she spoke, "Was the voice male or female?"

"Female," Eric responded.

"I heard her too," Gerry said.

Come to find out, two nights after Eric's incident, Gerry experienced the same thing.

The bar had been incredibly busy before the show. Gerry hadn't had time for a bathroom break before the crowd rushed in. It wasn't until the show started that she had time to slip away for a second. Knowing that people use the lounge restrooms during the show, she snuck off to the men's room upstairs. She had barely shut the stall door when the she heard a female voice shout, "GET OUT!"

It was clear and direct. Gerry didn't wait around for a second warning. She ran downstairs to use the facilities in the lounge.

The two of them seemed relieved to know that the voice wasn't in their heads; however, they were concerned with the level of urgency the woman had in her command.

Because of the experiences with this woman, I wonder if she is trying to protect us from the more malevolent spirit roaming around upstairs. Is it Minnie? Is it the waitress who was rumored to have been murdered? No one knows for sure.

CHAPTER
16

Costume Room

On the far left side of the upstairs, there are two double-doored entryways. On the left is the entrance to the large wardrobe and on the right is the entrance to the large prop room. You will find that this book does not contain a prop room chapter because no experience has been associated with it. Hard to believe that a theater this active has inactive rooms, but the prop room is that room in this building. However, the large rectangle room on the corner of the building with two windows, aka the costume room, is another story.

The windows have been covered for years and years preventing outside light from coming into the room. Why? I'm not sure. The only explanation I can think of is to protect the costumes from the sun's harmful, fade-inducing rays. Anyway, the windows are boarded up.

Packed to the gils with costumes from every era, this room is frequented mostly by Shawn, Robert, and me when we are looking for costume pieces for shows. Strangely, it's an incredibly inspiring room.

This area was believed to have been a bar when it was a NCO Club. Now, it sits quietly for long periods at a time standing guard for the timeless garments in its care.

Activity in this room varies from confusing to downright frightening. A common occurrence that has been reported since the seventies comes from patrons, employees, and volunteers. The reports come in forms of phone calls even people walking into the building.

"There is a man looking out the window at me," the person says.

The reports have become so frequent that someone made a cut-out of a woman and placed her in one of the windows of the room. While the silhouette was meant to make light of the situation, the experiences are very real.

While it would be easy to dismiss the reports as a glare from the sun or light hitting the window funny, figures have been seen looking out both windows at all times of day and night.

One night, Shawn was getting in his car and glanced up at the side window. There was a man looking back at him. Because he has just closed and knew no one was inside, he assumed his eyes were playing tricks on him. He got in his car and left. About halfway home, he realized that the window the man was looking out of was actually covered by a floor to ceiling show rack. There was no way a person could have gotten to the window to look out at him.

Footsteps

Footsteps are another regular occurrence heard throughout the theater. Their intensity varies according to area of the theater, but they are still there.

Florence told me that she was upstairs one evening with her friend Louis. They were standing in the hallway talking and could hear heavy footsteps walking near them in the hallway.

Strangely, the footsteps sounded like they were walking on tile not carpet. They both looked around and saw no one; however, the footsteps were there.

Florence shared an interesting tidbit with me. Prior to 1982, the upstairs didn't have carpet. It was 100% tile.

I, too, have heard the footsteps upstairs. One evening, I had to run upstairs to the costume room during intermission to grab an alternate dress for one of the performers because the zipper had broken on her show dress.

Sifting through dress options, I heard footsteps coming down the hallway. They sounded like high heels clicking on the linoleum tile. Kathleen, Seeley's mom, was often my partner in crime with costumes at the time. Naturally, I assumed she was coming to check on my progress.

As the footsteps got closer to the door, I yelled out my position and looked up to greet her. The footsteps reached the door and stopped.

Thinking that was strange that she didn't walk in and I didn't hear her walk away, I thought someone else was trying to be funny and scare me. Smiling to myself, I thought I'll scare them. I grabbed the replacement dress and quietly tiptoed toward the door. As I got close, I jumped out and said, "Boo!" Nothing. No one. I was alone.

I have no idea who the female footsteps belonged to, but the energy was not scary. In fact, I felt nothing at all.

"They're Coming"

One of the coolest pieces of evidence captured during paranormal investigations are EVPs or electronic voice phenomena. This gives unequivocal proof that a voice was heard and what it said.

I know, I know. I've watched all the television shows where a quick static-like blurb is heard and the host translates it as, "It's a demon and it's telling me it wants to kill me." Uh huh. Or is it just a static burst?

There are some EVPs though that are crystal clear. No matter how you look at it, the voice is undoubtedly saying exactly what we hear. This experience was one of those cases. While I did not hear the actual recording personally, Robert did. I have documented the event based on his testimony.

Paranormal happenings are pretty well-known among those of us that have spent any amount of time there. Of course, there are people that try to discount what we say or dismiss it as active imaginations. That's all fine and good. I don't need someone else to tell me what I have and haven't experienced in my life.

A group of musicians that used to perform at the Harlequin had a healthy interest in ghosts. Half the band were cautious believers while the other half were cautious skeptics.

After hearing some stories about activities reported upstairs, a few of them decided to go on an unofficial ghost hunt armed with a flashlight, a recorder, and a healthy dose of courage. They spent about thirty minutes upstairs and got nothing. Discouraged and admittedly bored, they decided to pull the plug on the hunt and head back down to finish rehearsal.

At the last minute, the wife of the drummer decided that she was going to leave the recorder on in the costume room just to see if the spirits would talk while the space was empty. The group waited as she turned the recorder back on and set it in a secure position; then they all made their way downstairs.

Because they had already been midway through rehearsal, they only spent an additional hour or so on stage. Rehearsal wrapped and they all said their goodbyes before leaving. Everyone tends the be exhausted after singing and dancing for hours, so they are in a hurry to get out of there.

With most of the group gone, there were only a few stragglers left in the building finishing up some notes and chatting about fixes. They all wrapped up and headed toward the door to leave. Suddenly, the drummer's wife remembered that she needed to get her recorder from upstairs. Because it was late and the lights were off upstairs, she had her husband walk up with her.

Luckily, the trip to grab the recorder was uneventful. The only thing memorable was the hearty laugh that she and her husband had as they went up the stairs. As they got to the room, she noticed that the recorder was switched off. She thought nothing of it assuming the tape ran out. Anxious to get out of there, she grabbed it and they headed out for the evening.

The next day, she remembered the recording. As she went about her daily chores, she listened to the sound of silence coming out of the speaker. Suddenly, she started to hear the sound of chatter. Her description likened the chatter to that of the atmosphere of a bar where multiple people are talking, but you can't really make out any of them. Next, she could hear a piano playing music.

Absolutely perplexed because there was not a piano anywhere nearby, she tried to listen closer. As she leaned in, the chatter and music stopped followed by the sound of her and her husband's laughter. She remembered that was when they were coming up the stairs.

In the silence, she could hear their footsteps coming down the hallway. Just as their footsteps reached the door, a female voice whispered, "They're coming," and the recorder stopped. She had to rewind the recording to listen to it again. Yes, it was really there and clearly audible.

"They're coming."

She realized a few things immediately: 1) the Harlequin ghost stories are very real, 2) there is more than one entity in the building, 3) it has the ability to touch things like the recorder, and 4) it can see us, too.

CHAPTER

17

The Office

Halfway down the upstairs hall is the door to the main office. Comprised of two rooms, the first room houses a futon and bookshelves that hold hundreds of scripts from over forty years of plays. Years ago the theater director, Bruce, used this room for auditions.

The second room has a desk, chair, and some additional bookshelves. Both rooms have very little decor albeit photographs of past productions. Because the room is no longer used, people rarely have a reason to enter it. Therefore, any reports of experiences in the room have been nearly nonexistent. That is with the exception of my experience.

Fast Talking Woman

As you learned in Chapter One, I started volunteering at the Harlequin during the 2009-2010 season. About this time, I was assigned the brilliant task of cleaning out the clutter in the office upstairs; then organizing the items that remained.

This task would have been excessive, even overwhelming for someone who didn't like a challenge, but they found the right person in me.

Paperwork was piled up all over with miscellaneous items stuffed everywhere.

With the cast rehearsing in the theater downstairs and the staff working in the first floor box office, I dove into the mountain of papers in the office. I had heard stories about strange things that happen in the theater, but I chose to put it out of my mind and focus on the task at hand.

It was early evening and I was completely engrossed in the elimination of unnecessary items. I could faintly hear the cast rehearsing the familiar songs of *Smokey Joe's Café*. I would sing along every once in awhile but for the most part, I wasn't really paying attention.

Suddenly, an unfamiliar voice began talking to me. Looking around to find the source of the sound, I stopped at the door of the ladies lounge across the hall. The voice was high pitched and clearly female. Her words were fast, jumbled and indistinguishable. It sounded as though they were being transported through a transistor radio from the fifties. The other strange observation was that the woman didn't stop to take a breath between her words.

I can't describe the feeling I felt initially. It wasn't fear - more like confusion. I stood looking around for what felt like an eternity. Before I even realized I was doing it, I spoke to her.

"I can't understand what you are saying. You're talking too fast. If you want to talk to me, slow down," I said.

It almost seemed like she knew I was listening to her because she became silent.

With the pile of things to finish in the office, I shrugged my shoulders and went about my business. To try to make the time go a little faster, I turned on my music and went back to work.

Within two minutes, she started talking again – faster and louder.

"I can't understand you. Please slow down," I repeated.

She kept talking at the same speed and the same frequency. Frustrated, I turned up the music to try to drown out her voice.

Apparently, that was not the right choice. Every time I increased the volume on my music, her voice got louder and her sense of urgency seemed to increase. I could almost feel her pleading with me to leave. Her words didn't convey a message, but their tone certainly did. My confusion quickly became anxiety.

I don't scare easily, but my intuition told me something wasn't right. Then I felt it. She was not the only spirit around me. The air started to thicken, the hair on the back of my neck stood up, and my fingers started to tingle.

I finally figured it out. She was warning me that something was coming. Unfortunately, I was too stubborn to listen. I wanted her message to come in a way that was comfortable for me, but she was telling me the only way she knew how. Finally, I understood.

"I got it. I'm outta here," I said as I grabbed my stuff and closed the doors.

"Thank you for looking out for me," I told her. Rushing down the hall to the stairs, I felt like something menacing was determined to push me out of that space while her energy had formed some sort of force field around me until I could leave.

When I reached the bottom of the stairs, the realization of what just happened hit me. For some reason, this spirit fought to protect me from some sort of evil on the other side. I don't know her name or her story, but I do know that she has been trapped with a negative male energy upstairs for God knows how long.

CHAPTER 18

Harlequin Spirits That Roam

I've done my best to compile activities in this book by the room the experience occurred in. I have found that people tend to connect better to the story if they can picture where it is happening. As with any location though, some strange activities are not isolated to one area of a building. They happen all over the place.

One strange occurrence that happens all over the theater is disembodied whistling which has been witnessed by many people; an experience that leaves the person who hears it more mystified than frightened. It happens randomly, never in the same place in the building. Robert and Antonio, another theater volunteer, heard it in the house while Shawn and Sarah have heard it in the lounge.

Another thing, I have found is that not all experiences with the

Harlequin spirits occur within the theater walls. If an entity feels a particular connection with a person, it just might follow that person home which can be terrifying. Unfortunately, several of us learned this the hard way.

Little Girl Followed Me Home

One of my favorite reasons for volunteering at the Harlequin was to work with the kids' group that performed there. Boys and girls in the age range of four to eighteen rehearsed twice every week, even more frequently if they were preparing for a show. I had the honor and privilege of working with these kids for several years. They were balls of energy, light, talent, and joy. Each one has inspired and continues to inspire me in a different way.

As with everything in life, things do not last forever and the group discontinued in 2013. One thing that remains is the love and pride I have for these children. They will never leave my heart.

One night after a particularly long dress rehearsal, we all gathered our things and headed to our individual homes.

Ashton and I spent our travel time in the car talking, singing, and just enjoying the time we had together. Because the rehearsal was long and we had to rest for the show the next day, we headed to bed as soon as we got home. I was exhausted and ready for a long nights sleep. I'm pretty sure I was asleep before my head hit the pillow.

At three o'clock in the morning, I awoke to the sound of screaming right beside my left ear. It was a little girl. I couldn't see her, but I could hear her. Her screams were of sheer excitement. She was ready to play. I just knew it was the little girl from the theater.

Sensing the energy, I could tell she meant no harm. She simply wanted me to know that she was here. Realizing the time and the fact that I had to get some sleep, I spoke to her.

"Oh, honey. I would love to play with you, but it is very important that you stay at the theater," I explained.

As soon as I said that, the room became silent, and the air changed. I knew her energy was gone, so I went back to sleep.

The next day, I was pondering about why she had followed me home. That's when it hit me. It was because I spent so much time at the theater interacting with the kids, listening to their songs, encouraging their talent, and supporting their every need. She saw me helping the kids at the theater and naturally assumed I would welcome her with open arms.

Obviously, I have no way to validate my assumption, but I have found a way to potentially justify why she followed me. Maybe I'm right, maybe I'm wrong. Either way, I feel good about how I handled my late night visitor.

It's in the Backseat

I can't tell you the number of times Ashton has told me that someone is in the car with us. In most cases, she just tells me to talk to her to take her mind off the backseat. Sometimes, the unknown passenger is seated behind her. Sometimes, it's behind me. One thing is for sure though - she will never turn around and under no circumstance will she look in the mirror. This time though was her most frightening experience.

One night after a show, we had just embarked on our thirty minute drive home from the Harlequin. As always, Ashton was singing along with her favorite songs. After driving about fifteen minutes, Ashton suddenly became quiet. She tensed up, and put her hands over her ears. I knew what it meant when she brought her hands to her ears, but this time she was far more agitated than I've ever seen her.

"What's wrong?" I asked.

She shook her head.

Many times, Ashton and I can feel presences at this same time. This time, I felt nothing. Confused, I began questioning her again.

"Honey....." I said.

I hadn't gotten more then one word out of my mouth before she began aggressively shaking her head again.

"Ash, what is it?" I asked.

"Don't talk about it," she said.

Now, I was really pissed. Something was messing with my little girl. It had systematically prevented me from being able to sense it and I wasn't able to talk about it. She could tell that I was getting frustrated.

Based on her eyes staring forward, I knew she sensed something in the backseat. I had never seen her this upset or frightened by energies before. Finally, she spoke.

"Make it go away."

I don't know the absolute solution to make a malicious entity go away, but I do know that saying The Lord's Prayer always helps. Without hesitating, I began reciting it to which Ashton quickly joined. Together, we must have said it non-stop twenty times. The more we chanted, the more empowered we felt.

Finally, we pulled into our garage. I could see the tension melt away from her face. Before we got out of the car, I asked her if she could tell me what the heck just happened.

Here is exactly what she told me:

"As we were driving along, I felt something looking at me from the seat behind you. I knew it wasn't good, so I kept fighting to keep it from entering my thoughts. It wanted me to look at it, but I wouldn't because I felt like it was going to attack me. The more I fought against it, the angrier it got," she said.

"What was it? What did it look like?" I asked.

"I didn't look at it, but I could tell it was about my size. It felt like it was a human person, but, there was something not normal about it," she responded.

"What do you mean it wasn't normal?"

She thought for a moment.

"I wouldn't say it was demonic but most definitely was more than just a mean person," she continued.

"What made you think it was mean?"

"I just knew. I can't explain it. It was getting angry because I wouldn't look at it. It's eyes were huge and focused on me. The angrier it got, the bigger the eyes were becoming. It tried to force it's thoughts on me, but I kept blocking them," she said.

I wanted to help calm her, but I could tell she needed to get the story out. She took a deep breath and continued.

"I tried to protect myself like you always tell me, so I surrounded myself in a bubble of God's white light and prayed in my head," she said.

"And that didn't work?" I asked.

"No. That just made it more mad. I don't know. It just made me feel really crazy, Mom," she said almost in disbelief.

She shook her head trying to rid herself of the memory, then spoke again.

"The biggest thing that stood out was its eyes. Those huge, frightening eyes," she explained.

I remember the night it happened. The entire experience lasted about ten minutes, but it felt like five hours.

Ashton revealed to me after telling me this story that she felt like if she looked directly the thing, it would have overtaken her.

To this day, she will tell you that was the most frightening experience she has ever had with the other side. Unfortunately for her, she has had more experiences than most people.

Robert's House

Robert has always been sensitive, but activity at his house was minimal for the most part. After he started working at the Harlequin, that all changed. While he could write a separate book on it, I wanted to share some of the things that he has been forced to witness over the past eight years.

Similar to activity at the theater, he regularly sees balls of light floating around without any explanation. He's tried everything he can think of to debunk it, but has not been able to. There is also no correlation as to when it happens. We always talk about writing it down to keep track, but life goes by quickly. We often forget.

The other thing that makes a regular appearance in his home is wispy, white smoke. Like the balls of light, there is no indicator as to when it will be appearing. It doesn't frighten him, it just gives him a slight jolt because he isn't expecting it.

I have to share another frequently occurring activity because I believe its validation of a presence in his home.

Robert's dogs play with someone. He's actually recorded it. The dogs dance around reacting to something just as they would to a normal human. None of the canines are afraid in any way. As a matter of fact, they seem to love the attention of this unseen entity or entities. This doesn't happen all the time but enough to indicate there is a spirit that comes in and out of his home. Could things be following him home too?

Strange Activity

Theater lovers enjoy being a part of the action in any way they can be. They don't have to sing or act to be a part of it. Some choose to donate vintage clothes, knick knacks, even furniture that can be used for costumes, props, or set pieces. These donations can be critical to the success of a community theater because many run 100% on volunteers and charitable gifts.

Some time ago, someone dropped off items for the theater including a halogen lamp. It required some cleaning and paint touch ups. Wanting to get it done quickly, Shawn took it home to finish the refresh. He arrived home and sat the lamp in the corner of his guest room.

Around this time, the Harlequin performers were asked to participate in another event for a local non-profit company. Because Shawn coordinates the participation for activities outside the theater, he put the light refresh on hold temporarily.

He spent approximately two weeks on the non-profit project and all the while, the light sat looking at him from the guest room.

One night, he was editing music at his table. Suddenly, the light fell over on its own as though someone got behind it and pushed it. The crash startled him and his dogs who were laying at his feet. He walked into the guest room and saw nothing that would have caused the unexpected tip of the light. He shrugged it off as a fluke.

Within a few days, he had forgotten about the incident until he was getting ready to go to work. Running late, he stopped momentarily when he noticed his green hat that had gone missing the week before. It was sitting on the table in the living room. Confused, he walked over to it. Just as he reached the table, he felt an air breeze behind his head then a loud crash hit the wall beside him.

He turned to look. On the floor, he saw the blue tea lights that had been sitting on another table across the room. They were shattered in pieces from being thrown against the wall by an invisible source. Not wanting to find out what caused it, he grabbed his keys and left.

Like the green hat, things disappear and reappear all the time at Shawn's house. He's lost track of all the items that have done this. One that he can always count on is Christmas decorations.

Every year without fail, something disappears then reappears days sometimes weeks later in plain sight.

Dark Mass at my House

Many times rehearsals run late, so there are times that I'm hungry when I get home. One night, Ashton and I got home and decided we wanted macaroni and cheese. It's our family's staple food. Eric was traveling so, I told Ash to run up and take a shower while I made dinner.

Cooking in my kitchen is usually normal with the exception of the dining room which you can see from the stove area. On occasion several of my family members, including me, have seen shadows moving about in there regardless of day or night. Because I was so hungry this night, shadows were the last thing on my mind.

Noticing the water boiling, I dumped the noodles in the pan and began to stir. Suddenly, a feeling of dread came over me. A voice in my head kept telling me not to look in the dining room. Fighting the urge to look was difficult. I had to walk away from the stove several times. Finally, I had no choice but to go back to the cooking noodles. I was surprised at how well I was able to prevent myself from looking into the dining room.

Draining the noodles, adding the butter, then adding the cheese, I managed to get through it all. But then I turned to grab two bowls out of the cabinet and looked directly into the room. My eyes immediately saw what my instinct was desperately trying to prevent me from seeing.

A black shadow mass approximately three and a half feet high stood across the table beside my dining room chair. There were no features at all. It looked like a swirling black mass of smoke. I just stood there paralyzed. It didn't move from its spot, it just swirled within itself. Something in me shook me out of my paralysis and I switched on the dining room light. The black mass disappeared instantly.

Frightened, I texted Robert to tell him about my experience. I needed to share it with someone that I knew has seen the black mass at the theater and someone who wouldn't think I was completely crazy.

After a couple of holy shits, he was able to calm me down before Ashton got back downstairs. I still ate the mac and cheese. Even scary, swirling black masses won't rob me of that wonderful experience.

CHAPTER 19

The Harlequin Today

The Harlequin continues to proudly present well-known plays and original musical revues with some of the same people that you met in this book. The theater is thriving and receives excellent reviews from *Broadway World* as well as the *San Antonio Express News*.

This incredible building has been standing for over eighty years. I am honored to be a part of its past, present, and future. It truly is a magical place even without the supernatural phenomena.

Unexplained occurrences continue whether we are there to witness them or not. We don't know everything that triggers activity, but we are aware of some things.

First, the spirits seem to like music from the fifties. From the time rehearsals begin through the last curtain call in fifties shows, the activity picks up. There is no explanation as to why; it just does. That said, there are some days during those rehearsals that nothing happens.

The other trigger seems to be plays with heavy drama in them. Murder mysteries, *The Gingerbread Lady*, *The Bad Seed*, and *The Birds* seemed to be the worst. Some of the most terrifying moments occurred before and after these shows.

One thing for sure is that they work on their time, not ours. They aren't a circus act and they make their appearance when they see fit.

While I was writing this book, I found it interesting that paranormal activity around me had picked up. Because I completed most of my writing at my house, that was the first place I noticed activity increasing. From waking up to a presence in the bedroom to unexplained movements, things were happening. Even my dog was growling at shadows.

One night, Eric and I were watching a movie in the living room while Ashton worked on her homework upstairs. During a commercial break, Eric muted the television to talk to me.

Before he opened his mouth to speak, we could hear movement in the kitchen. It sounded like someone was moving something heavy across the room. We looked at each other then walked into the kitchen to look around. Finding nothing, we shook our heads and went back to the living room.

Our butts were barely in their seats when we heard the sound again. Frustrated, Eric looked at me.

"Finish that damn book," he said.

I laughed and assured him that I was working as fast as I could.

Another example occurred at the theater. I met Shawn and Robert one afternoon for a set build. After working for a few hours on the stage, I sat down to gather some details from them about the experiences I had drafted so far.

That night, Robert sent me a text to tell me that he was hearing disembodied voices and strange noises all evening at the theater. I'm not sure if this happens to others when they document accounts of the paranormal, but it happened to me.

Maybe it was just coincidence. Either way, it won't chase me away from a place that I love.

After I thought this book was completed, the Harlequin produced a murder mystery in February 2017 called *Deathtrap* with a small cast of four. Throughout the show, the cast heard various reports of paranormal activity at the theater. Because each cast member was a skeptic, they took these accounts with a grain of salt. That was until closing weekend.

As they progressed through the three shows that weekend, one by one the cast members caught glimpses of a male figure backstage. One night, it waved to one of the female actresses.

Another night, it was peering out from behind a curtain on stage left at one of the male actors. Luckily this time, the entity was playful not frightening. This leads me to believe the figure they saw was not the shadow man. Is there a new entity now?

It's hard to tell. Either way, he made his presence known so that he would have a small voice in the book. I'm happy to say he got it.

Through the doors of the Harlequin have welcomed generations of performers, volunteers, patrons and military personnel. We have formed life long friendships and lost some of our closest friends along the way.

The Harlequin is like no other theater that I have ever seen. We have worked hard to create and foster an atmosphere of love, support, and encouragement. Because of the strength in our connections, I know our bond will stand the test of time. We are a real family - the Harlequin family.

Of course, the Harlequin spirits are just as much a part of our family as the living. We welcome everyone to stop in for a quick visit, hit the lounge for a drink, or stay for a show. This is what a "real theater" feels like.

Drop in if you dare. Just kidding...... or am I?

Until next time

ACKNOWLEDGMENTS

The stories compiled in this book are collected from people that have experienced the activities first-hand. They are true and documented to the best of my abilities. While this book outlines numerous incidents that occurred at the Harlequin, it only scratches the surface as to what we all experience on a regular basis.

Recounting these stories were sometimes as frightening as experiencing them. What the reader did not see is the activity that kicked up anytime and anywhere the stories were being discussed as this book was taking form. It was as if the spirits wanted to remind us of their presence through moving objects, darting shadows, and unexplained footsteps.

Additionally, the blood, sweat, and tears associated with writing a book like this is an incredible investment that is never completed singlehandedly. With that, I owe an immeasurable amount of gratitude to every single person identified in the next two pages.

Eric, Ashton, Kirstin, Molly, Caleb, Sarah, Mom, & Dad - Thank you all for your continuous love, support, and encouragement. You never allowed me to give up. I love you.

Robert, Shawn, and Todd & Ally Crookshank - Thank you for being the most amazing friends in the universe. Your patience with my constant questions and incessant talking is truly appreciated. I love you.

Melissa Dean, Andrea Howard, Ian O'Regan, Robert Olivas, Faye Joki & June Gossler Anderson - From concept to completion, you were all there to help guide me with helpful direction and honest feedback. Thank you for being my behind the scenes superheroes.

My Harlequin family (you know who you are) - Thank you for sharing your love, light, incredible talent and amazing friendship. Love y'all.

Dave Schrader & Greg Lawson - Thank you for inspiring me to write this book during our ten day adventure through the Emerald Isle. You're the best.

Barry Klinge & Brad Klinge - Thank you for your validations, expertise, and for letting me tag along on your investigations. Can't wait until the next one.

Karson Kelley & Sammy Ochoa - You are missed every single day and will be forever in our hearts. Know that there is always a spot on stage for both of you. ~Just Love~

Fort Sam Houston - Thank you for allowing the Harlequin to entertain audiences season after season. I'm proud to volunteer at such a wonderful place.

Harlequin patrons and friends - Thank you for your never-ending kindness and support. You have no idea how important you are to all of us.

Thank you to following individuals for giving the spirits a voice and most importantly, trusting me to share it. *Ashton, Eric, Shawn, Robert, Florence Bunton, Johnny Halpenny, Gerry Parisi, Sarah Peters, Katie Molina, Garrett Scot Henry, Melissa Dean, Dave Dean, Matthew Kjos, Samantha Eberle, Kylee Skye Lynn, Lisa Valle, Jenn Harris, Michael Zaiontz, Yleana Wooten, Matt Tejeda, Nicki Martinez, Suzy Bianchi, Dorin Finn, and Steve Brophy.*

NIKKI FOLSOM

ABOUT THE AUTHOR

Nikki lives in San Antonio, Texas with her husband, daughter, and sweet canine boy. She loves traveling, writing, photography, theatre, and spending time with those she loves. While paranormal experiences cannot always be explained, she remains a loyal and committed volunteer to the Harlequin and her Harlequin family.

Because she has always been intrigued by the unexplained, Nikki plans to continue investigating, researching, and writing about other haunted locations from all around the globe. In fact, her next book will documenting the paranormal experiences throughout her life.

24788206R00119

Made in the USA
Columbia, SC
30 August 2018